ings, on the outside is Les Spangler, Behind Cummings is National champion
arvey Ward's No. 5 Miller. Ernie Triplett trails Brunmier. (Alvarez-Craig photo).

LEGION
ASCOT SPEEDWAY
(1920s-1930s)

By

John R. Lucero

ORECUL PUBLISHING COMPANY

P.O. Box 2154   Downey, CA 90242

DEDICATED

To the thousands of kids who didn't have the fifty cents to get in . . . but who never missed a race.

Also dedicated to the following men who, from time to time, served as racing officials and helped make Ascot a standout attraction:

Ralph DePalma, 1915 Indianapolis winner; Tommy Milton, 1921-23 Indianapolis winner; Earl Cooper, three-time National AAA champion; Capt. Eddie Rickenbacker, World War I flying ace, former president of the Indianapolis Motor Speedway, and early day racing driver; veteran board track drivers Harry Hartz and Leon Duray; pioneer racing driver Eddie Pullen; veteran drivers Cliff Bergere, Frank Verbeck, Cliff Durant and Frank Elliott; veteran driver Eddie Meyer, contestant in Ascot's first-ever race; and record breaking, barnstorming driver Barney Oldfield.

And to former athletes who served as honorary judges and made trophy presentations, such as heavyweight boxing champion Jack Dempsey, world wrestling champion Ed "Strangler" Lewis, All-American halfback Irving "Cotton" Warburton of USC fame, the late Johnny Mack Brown, All-American halfback from the University of Alabama and later a motion picture star, and to the many motion picture lovelies who presented trophies and the Victory Crown Helmet to winning drivers of the Italian Helmet Dash.

TABLE OF CONTENTS

ACKNOWLEDGMENTS

Credit should be given to the persons mentioned herein, for without their cooperation and assistance in providing facts about Ascot history and other data, this true story could not have been written. My thanks to:

• Dr. Fred Loring, head of the Racing Board, American Legion Post 127, Glendale, California. (Dr. Loring died on November 15, 1975, at age 89, five days after being interviewed!)

• Harry Schmidt, American Legion Post 127, Glendale, California, for many years superintendent of the Ascot track.

• Edwin W. Austin, American Legion Post 127, Glendale, California, for many years general manager of Ascot Speedway.

• Norman J. Hartford, Ascot's ace publicity writer of 1929-32 (deceased).

• E. H. "Roscoe" Turner, veteran automobile racing historian and collector, whose encouraging remark, "You have undying determination," inspired the author to complete the book and have it published.

• W. S. (Bill) White (deceased), Ascot promoter and owner of the famous "Red Lion Special" which Ernie Triplett drove to the 1931-32 Pacific Coast championship.

• Dick Goodfellow, veteran Ascot fan who resides in Portland, Oregon.

• Veteran driver Eddie Meyer, (deceased) who drove in Ascot's first race and whose brother Louis won the Indianapolis 500 in 1928, 1933, 1936.

• Mrs. Rex (Dorothy) Mays, widow of the 1934-1935 Pacific Coast AAA and 1940-1941 National AAA champion.

• Paul Weirick and Art Sparks, who built Al Gordon's 1933 championship car, the "Sparks-Weirick Miller Special" and holder of the all-time Ascot one-lap record.

• Oscar "Red" Garnant, mechanic on many Ascot cars and brother of the late car owner-mechanic Russ Garnant.

• Mrs. Gertrude Dorcey (deceased) and husband Al Dorcey, who contributed Pacific Southwest champion Francis Quinn's scrapbook, from which many facts were obtained.

• Doug Boyd, of Burbank, California, a former Ascot fan and collector of Ascot mementos.

• Thanks to my two dear aunts, Mrs. Albert Zaldatte and Mrs. Elvira Lucero, for encouraging the author to complete the book.

• Les Quinn, of Alhambra, brother of the 1930 Pacific Southwest champion Francis Quinn.

Other former Ascot drivers:

• Babe Stapp (deceased), Ed Winfield, Mel Kenealy, (1929 Pacific Southwest champion), Chris Vest, Mel McKee (deceased), Joe Crocker, Bob Scovel, Arvol Brunmier (deceased), Kelly Petillo, winner of the 1935 Indianapolis 500 (deceased), (Bert Spencer (deceased).

• Thanks also to the late Jack Buxton and 1928 Pacific Southwest champion, later Ascot's staff artist, whose numerous head size line drawings of fellow drivers delighted the fans, some of which are included in the book's illustrations.

• And above all, utmost gratitude for the blessings which made the author's childhood dreams come true.

ABOUT THE AUTHOR . . .

Enjoyable
reading
and
Best
Wishes
to
Frank J. Uhl
Jr.

Sincerely

(Photo Rick Corrales, L.A. Times)

AUTHOR JOHN LUCERO

John Lucero
Dec. 10, 1990

Ever stand alongside a sleek looking racing car, stare at the driver in awe and admire his driving style? I'm sure present day racing fans have been thrilled by this experience.

I received my "racing baptismal" as a child back in the early 1930s. Watching speeding racers at old Ascot Speedway in my hometown of Los Angeles, was a thrill I'll never forget. People were hungry, many were jobless, the depression was upon us, but the attraction of Ascot apparently helped keep us interested in life.

As for standing alongside a racing car, I sure did—many times. Only a few Fronty Fords remained when I emerged upon the Ascot scene; most of the cars were very classy looking "Miller Specials" loaded with nickel plating and painted the brightest of colors.

I stood alongside the cars of Mel Kenealy, Bryan Saulspaugh, Bill Cummings, Al Gordon, Francis Quinn, Ernie Triplett, "Stubby" Stubblefield, Kelly Petillo, Rex Mays, Harris Insinger, Chet Gardner—on the track and in the pits.

I recall my first visit to Ascot. It was a Saturday afternoon in 1930 when my brother Joe, eldest of the Lucero boys, took me to watch the drivers practice for the following day's races. A spin-out by car No. 99 on the north turn thrilled me. The car was the yellow colored "Hooker Special" driven by Ed Winfield, although my brother, thinking it was Pete DePaulo at the time, yelled, "That's Pete DePaulo."

You see, in those days, and up until the track's closure in 1936, the Ascot management let the fans in free on Saturdays to watch the cars hot-lapped and tuned for Sunday racing. Free admission was also allowed on Tuesday nights for Wednesday night racing. In this way the fans became acquainted with cars and drivers which inspired promotional success.

To me Ascot offered the most glorious setting of all sports, certainly the most thrilling of my life. The track highlighted the fastest and prettiest cars and the best drivers; best promotion by the AAA and American Legion; offered a terrific view from the 12,000 seat grandstand; featured the most glamorous motion picture starlets, who presented the trophy and a sweet kiss to winners of the "Italian Helmet Dash;" heart-throbbing races; 100 and 250 lap main events on Sundays and 50 and 75 lappers on Wednesday night on the 5/8 mile track.

I feel very fortunate to have attended the races there for almost six consecutive years. Young as I was, I can still remember the best of auto racing. Ascot had class . . . had color . . . had it all!

I was born in the northeastern suburb of Los Angeles known as Lincoln Heights, about four miles from Ascot. At night we could hear the roar of racing motors while tucked in bed.

Our mother, who died in 1928, left four sons and a daughter. My sister and brothers, my father and two terrific aunts raised me. Since Ascot by 1930 was in its heydey, my brothers would take me to the track to see Ernie Triplett, Walt May, Arvol Brunmier, Jimmy Sharp, Francis Quinn, "Stubby" Stubblefield and others perform at alarming, dizzy speeds.

Francis Quinn was 1930 Pacific Southwest champion and became the hero of our neighborhood because he lived in Lincoln Heights . . . four blocks from the Lucero household. The "Bald Eagle" was held in high esteem. On Broadway and Sichel Street was Ray Rapp's garage where Quinn stored and worked on his classy $6,000 No. 1 speedster powered by a Miller Marine engine.

We kids visited the garage many times to peek at the gold numeraled, pale blue

"Francis Quinn Special." That was in 1931. Francis always welcomed us in a friendly way . . . never turned us down. Our neighborhood became the center of gloom when Quinn was fatally injured in a highway accident in December. The loss of the highly admired and beloved Quinn was a hard blow for we kids to endure.

Quinn's number was retired in his honor for the remainder of the season and racing continued at Ascot. Me, my brothers Joe, Charley and Eddie, an uncle, my cousins and countless friends remained Ascot fans despite the death of the "Bald Eagle."

At Ascot there was a row of trees outside the south turn. One tree was called the "Lucero-Donahue tree" which was constantly occupied by my brothers and our friends, the Donahues, to watch the program for free. There was also a huge water tank on the main parking lot and even taller trees outside the south turn which older guys climbed to watch the races. Police on horseback patrolled the north turn hillside to keep kids out of the dangerous area.

Ever sneak into the races? We did plenty of times. To me there was no greater thrill than to sneak in at Ascot and catch the "Helmet" Dash" and main event. Believe me, when you saw such drivers as Triplett, Mays, Cummings, Petillo, Carey, Gordon, Stapp, Shaw and Saulspaugh on the same track, you were seeing something. Just as astounding was the earlier day attraction of Triplett, Quinn, Walt May, Brunmier, Sharp, Shortly Cantlon and Herman Schurch.

I saw Al Gordon and Spider Matlock crash to their deaths in Ascot's last race. I also saw Tommy Newton, Babe Stanyer, Bud Snavely and Bob Carey receive their final checkered flag. Those were awesome sights and I grieve over their loss. When Al

Gordon died, I wept as much when Francis Quinn died.

My brothers saw H. D. (Hal) Provan, Herman Schurch, George Young, Earl Farmer, Kenny Morgan, Tom Forsythe and Kenny Stoddard killed at Ascot. Bob Carey's death I recall most vividly. Carey was doing about 115 mph entering the north turn when, it was echoed through the grandstand, the throttle on his car became stuck. No time to shut her off . . . wham . . . into the steel rail. When they extricated Carey from the car, the National AAA champion was near death. Years later I met the barber who gave Carey his final haircut. "Slow her down, Bob," the barber said, as he cautioned the Anderson, Indiana, driver. But Carey was determined to break Al Gordon's one-lap record. He almost did, too, in the Joe Marks 270 cu. in. Miller from Garey, Indiana.

In those days the sleek looking, open cockpit and fishtail racing cars gave the fans the opportunity to study a driver's style. For instance:

Francis Quinn crouched over the steering wheel while peering over the cowl like a bulldog. He was a leadfoot all the way . . . "the best," said Ed Winfield.

Ernie Triplett held his head erect, his shoulders pressed slightly forward, picturesquely clad in white helmet and red sweater while manipulating the stunning "Red Lion Special." A masterful driver.

Bill Cummings was a spectacular driver. I can still see his arms whipping in the wind, steaming through a turn, his white shirt sleeves rolled up and his shirt-tail caught in the slipstream. "Wild Bill" did things spectacularly on a race track.

Bob Carey was a classy looking driver who sat calmly, his back rested comfortably against the back seat with arms extended like a chauffeur driving down main street. He could shoot through the turns with the slightest effort . . . a light touch of the wheel.

Rex Mays whipped his arms colorfully. He'd "set 'em up and take 'em" smoothly and convincingly.

Al Gordon just crouched over, "stood on it" courageously, and let 'er rip, while driving the "Sparks-Weirick Miller Special" to dizzy heights.

Floyd Roberts bent slightly over the steering wheel. He was big and burly . . . barely fit in a racing car.

Kelly Petillo, like Carey, appeared calm in the cockpit while passing his rivals with ease.

Shorty Cantlon was so short they sometimes placed cushions inside the cockpit of his Ascot car so hc could see over the hood.

Bryan Saulspaugh was all guts, aggressor and a death defying driver. He'd whip his car around the Ascot oval like a general in full command.

Louie Meyer was a master driver—calm and intelligent . . . tooled his car effortlessly . . . a true professional. Look around at the drop of the checkered flag and you'll see Louie among the front-runners.

Chet Gardner was a "money driver" and a heady one. He always seemed to be among the front-runners when the checkered flag was dropped at the finish of a race.

Carl Ryder was the "wild man" of the speedway. Many times he was all over the track, relentlessly storming toward the front.

Harris Insinger was so handsome one would believe he'd pursue a motion picture career. But Harris loved auto racing, and his colorful attire and splendid driving ability earned him the plaudits of the racing fans.

We always considered Arvol Brunmier the "ace" of Ascot. Muscular, mustachoed, good-looking, Arvol was always in the front-running. A terror on the track, he was ac-

tually married on the home stretch!

Les Spangler liked to peer at the fans in the grandstand while receiving a kiss from a starlet after winning one of his numerous "Helmet Dash" races. Les lost his life at Indy in 1933, and Ascot fans took an emotional beating.

The prettiest car I ever stood alongside was Earl Haskell's 220 cu. in. Miller No. 18 which was driven by Mel Kenealy in 1933. That jet black car with nickel plated front end, oil pressure pump, brake handle, exhaust pipe and spoked wheels, was a beautiful creation. The car shone brightly with its silver numeral.

I also stood alongside Russ Garnant's No. 12 Miller driven by Harris Insinger; Triplett's No. 1 owned by Bill White, Al Gordon's No. 5 built by Art Sparks and Paul Weirick, and Quinn's No. 1 Miller Marine at Ray Rapp's garage. To me, Kenealy's No. 18, with its beautiful lines was the prettiest of them all. This car later became Ted Horn's "Baby" in Eastern and Midwestern campaigns.

My family kept memorable scrapbooks about Ascot . . . the victories, the action, the fatalities . . . all lasting memories that would one day inspire me to write the history of the track. Service in the Navy during World War II did not deter my ambition. After my discharge I began to gather data and acquire photographs for this book.

The deaths of Al Gordon and Spider Matlock in 1936 saddened me. I became more despondent when promoter Bill White closed the track . . . probably due to the many deaths and adverse publicity.

One day I walked the four miles to Ascot. I found the grandstand burned to the ground. Only the oval remained with weeds sprouting through the dirt-oil surface.

Sadly I walked around the entire track hoping that someone would promote racing again. It was not to be and only lasting memories would I retain. I was remembering Ascot . . .

Imagine, I was a mere 10-year-old boy, not realizing that 45 years later I would write the history of this electrifying and magnificent track.

Hopefully I have accomplished my ambition: To "put the reader on the track" and to captivate the racing fan with the magic name of ASCOT!

John Lucero

INTRODUCTION

The automobile racing driver—that unique breed of mankind—what inspired him to risk his life on what was perhaps the most dangerous track in the history of auto racing?

What daring passion pushed him along the "comeback trail" after a shattering wreck on that track almost snuffed out his life?

What possessed him to accept the chilling challenge of the track, where the fatality rate was higher than most tracks, its size, combined?

And finally, why did this daring driver bravely step inside his racing car, speed down the straightaways and through its tricky curves to satisfy his passion for speed, while fully realizing that he might be the next victim of the Grim Reaper?

All of these challenges and dangers existed on old Ascot Speedway's pebbly and slippery dirt-oil surface, where fearless drivers zipped along at 90 miles per hour on tires no wider than those used on passenger autos of the day . . . inadequate to control the thundering cars while cornering at speeds that were to increase up to 120 miles per hour!

Those were the challenges put to many courageous drivers at Ascot, which opened more than 50 years ago in the vicinity of Alhambra in Los Angeles County.

Ascot!"—that magic name in auto racing—might have made many of today's drivers wince and shudder with anxiety and apprehension (in many cases, fear) had they been faced with the same precarious challenge that confronted the intrepid Knights of the Roaring Road of the period between 1924 and 1936.

(Note: fear, apprehension and anxiety certainly would apply to today's self-styled "world champion" drivers of Europe, for only a fraction, if any, compete on the rugged USAC circuit which once was the AAA).

The Ascot track, long gone now, is considered by many veteran drivers, mechanics and oldtime officials (there are few left) as the most highly competitive and most hazardous speedway in the annuls of automobile racing.

"Ascot was a killer," they still mutter. Why? Because primitive equipment caused many wrecks: makeshift chassis were tough to handle, narrow tires blew repeatedly, broken spindles were common. Also, crash helmets did not exist; roll bars, seat belts and shoulder harnesses and roll cages were unheard of, yet the drivers possessed the iron will to win on a track that played no favorites when it rang the "death bell." These death-defying speed demons always vowed, "It can't happen to me."

When the boys took to Ascot's five-eighth's mile track many knew that their's was a race against death, that the outcome could result in their final rites, or a severe maiming, while battling other cloth helmeted gas pushers for modest earnings during those unpredictable depression years that followed.

Perhaps the name of the game would be death for most of the racing idols who participated there . . . who put their nerve on the line for the thrill of speed and victory, but unfortunately, resulted in death too often.

One might ask the question which has been asked a million times:

"Why risk life and limb while knowing full well what the end result might be?"

It's the same old answer:

"The lust for speed is a part of the noble racing driver's character. It is his way of life to meet the challenge of speed, no matter how dangerous the track—no matter how primitive his racing equipment might be. Speed and challenge is in his blood. He is obsessed with the passion for speed and daringness. Take away this passion and he is nothing!"

Ascot Speedway offered such a challenge to many an intrepid racing driver who defied death . . . stared the Grim Reaper in the eye and took frightening chances to prove that "he can't take me."

Yet, few of the many drivers who challenged the spectre of death enjoyed the taste of victory on Ascot's sometimes angry speedpaths.

Angry speedpaths, we say? Yes, considering the death toll, the old track seemed to angrily fight off the challenging drivers as its slippery banked curves and rapid straightaways were snuffing out a life or sending a brave driver to the hospital with multiple injuries.

This question also can be asked, however: Was Ascot really that dangerous?

Oldtime driver Eddie Meyer who drove in Ascot's first race, says "it was no more dangerous than any other track . . . the only dangers were an iron guardrail stretched along the north turn and the steep bank over the south turn where many cars took a rolling tumble. That was dangerous too. Why they ever put that iron rail along the north turn and why they never filled that bank on the south turn I'll never know."

But former Ascot track superintendent Harry Schmidt claims the oval was extremely dangerous because of its pebbly surface high along the fence which would cause many a nervy driver to skid wildly and out of control. Schmidt also cited human error on part of the drivers. "I should say that the guys took too many unbelievable chances while driving primitive cars which, many times, were defective."

Regardless, Ascot, "King of the Speedways," can lay claim to no less than 24 deaths during 13 heart stopping years.

It was promoter George R. Bentel and publicist William H. (Bill) Pickens who conceived the idea of building a speedy track that would feature smaller cars (lesser engine displacement) than those driven at Indianapolis and on the national one-mile circuits. The pair financed the five-eighth's mile Ascot track after a larger track, which was on the other side of town and with the same Ascot name, had yielded to industrial progress.

Bentel and Pickens had envisioned success. They were right . . . but neither realized that Ascot would produce champion drivers, become the scene of spectacular accidents, and be the awesome site of gory and fatal wrecks and that its controversy would create a wave of indignation among some drivers and track officials. It would be the press that would arouse public resentment and cause the legendary track to close its gates—forever.

"Ascot, King of the Speedways," opened as a dusty road course and oval, thanks to land leases and several gambling dollars. Despite a rough start, Ascot was to blossom into the most successful racing plant of its kind, among the type that stage weekly shows.

Under the sanction of International Motor Contest Association (IMCA), Ascot lured barnstorming drivers and many other devil-may-care "outlaw" pilots who vowed to race for fame and fortune on a track that was not yet refined. Some of the cars that were driven during the early years were

Duesenbergs, Whippets, the Essex, Delage, Frontenacs, Fiats and hopped-up Model T Fords equipped with Rajo heads. There also were some rickety stock and modified speed creations that only a gutty human would dare drive. Many were tail-less with their gasoline tanks vulnerable to puncture in otherwise wild tangles with other cars. A driver took his life into his hands.

Operating later under American Automobile Association (AAA) sanction and with American Legion-backed promotions, Ascot fame was to spread throughout the land . . . its sparkling racing cars, snappy looking track officials and pit crewmen, re-splendent racing drivers and motion picture stars who became faithful fans, gave Ascot that certain something called C-L-A-S-S.

Perhaps the capivating and colorful history of Ascot Speedway can be defined in five simple words:

A—acceleration. S—suspense. C—courage. O—obsession. T—thrills.

One thing is for certain, it is difficult to find the equal of this legendary track.

Those who attended the races there will support this statement, we are sure.

For Ascot was "King of the Speedways."
Read on and see why . . .

John Lucero

CHAPTER I

BENTEL'S DUSTY BOWL

(1924 - 1926)

Rajos! Frontys! Duesenbergs!

Cloth Helmets, Goggled Eyes

A Flying Start

Eddie Meyer Protests

DePalma's Victory Crown

The "Wisconsin Special"

Sensational Frank Lockhart

The Targo Florio

A Human "Cannonball"

Norris Shears Crashes

Hard Times, Tough Dollars

The day: January 20, 1924.

The place: New Ascot Motor Speedway, Los Angeles, California.

The event: Three-lap Italian Helmet Dash.

The drivers: Ralph DePalma, Fred Horey, Eddie Meyer, and Fred Leickleider.

Twelve thousand fans have crowded the new and huge grandstand extending along the main straightway, another three thousand are lining the infield parking area, standing on cars, and a few hundred more are sitting in rickety autos on a slightly sloped hill outside the north turn fence.

A row of trees which overlook the dangerous south turn is a "ringside seat" for many youngsters who don't have the half-buck to get in.

Zoom . . . the four daredevils get off on a flying start at the drop of starter Paul K. C. Durkham's green flag. (Durkham, a racing promoter from Bakersfield, was brought in for the special event).

Little Eddie Meyer takes the lead in his "Rajo Special" No. 4, with the white clad DePalma at his tail in a white, 8-cylinder "Miller Special" No. 1. Suddenly, down the backstretch Meyer plants a heavy foot on the throttle and after two more laps flashes to victory as the crowd cheers. Meyer, a five-year veteran of the roaring road, had just won the first-ever race on that memorable race track, with DePalma right at his rear wheels.

But wait!

DePalma steers his big Miller into the pits, alights from the car and strolls slowly towards the official starting line where he begins to file a protest. DePalma claims Meyer jumped the starting flag and got an unfair advantage.

The officials, siding with DePalma after group consultations, decide to re-run the race after declaring the previous start no contest.

Off to another start, this time DePalma rapidly takes the lead in the big Miller. Never headed, DePalma pushes the throttle to the floorboards and flashes to victory in the first official race on the Ascot track.

Zoom . . . zoom . . . zoom. Meyer, in his Model-T Ford "Rajo Special," Leickleider in an 8-cylinder Duesenberg and Horey in a Frontenac Ford finished not far behind De-Palma.

That was the unveiling of the famous Ascot Speedway some 65 years ago. It also was the beginning of a 13-year existence which was to see the track attain racing immortality.

Those first races ran under the auspices of Ascot Speedway Association and under the rules and sanction of the International Motor Contest Association (IMCA).

The crowd had roared its approval, Ascot had made an impressive debut and gave an indication of the type of action to be seen in future seasons.

The fans had come to see DePalma, winner of the 1915 Indianapolis 500 race and National Champion. And DePalma didn't let them down.

Ralph coasted the big Miller down the front straightaway in view of the grand-stand crowd and halted the machine at the judge's stand. There he accepted victory with a smile and received a thunderous ovation. The three-time AAA National Champion then waved to the crowd in token of appreciation. A disappointed Meyer looked on admiringly.

Moments later, the Vai Brothers emerged from the pits with their glowing and decorative creation—the Victory Crown Helmet.

After a brief announcement, they gently placed the crown on DePalma's graying head. The stands shook with excitement.

The Vai Brothers, who owned a winery in Cucamonga, California, had ordered the helmet made to honor their Italian countryman for his many victories over the years on many tracks throughout the U.S.

With the first-ever race at Ascot being the Dash for the four fastest qualifiers and with DePalma the winner, the Vai Brothers had a two-fold reason for presenting him with the ostentatious helmet. The presentation became a colorful tradition to spur future drivers to victory. The Victory Crown symbolized honor, especially for DePalma. Today the silver and gold plated headpiece is valued at $25,000.

But there was more action and thrills in store that opening day.

DePalma sat out the next race but came back to win his heat, and then sent the fans home happy by winning the 30-lap feature in a scorching duel with Fred Frame, Leon Duray and Horey. Also losers were Leickleider, Al Hopp, "Fuzzy Davidson, Eddie Winfield, Sig Haughdahl, Jack Petticord, "Pop" Evans and "Cannonball" Baker.

Famous dirt track driver "Babe" Stapp, who was to become a regular Ascot competitor and a 13-time entry at Indianapolis Speedway, broke a hub on his "Sherman Special" speedster and disappointedly sat out the entire program.

The partisan crowd wanted to see DePalma win, but they also wanted to watch the fired-up Model Ts, Fiats, Duesenbergs, "Fronty" Fords, Whippets, Delages, Jewetts, Essex and the few available others against the more refined Millers of DePalma and Duray. But in the end, DePalma's proved the superior mount and dusted off the others, some of which caried two men (driver and mechanic).

All of the cars during those barnstorming days were equipped with rear brakes only. (Four wheel brakes were a few years away from being introduced; disc brakes weren't even a dream).

As for tires, the ancient Model-Ts and "Frontys" and the expensive Millers had inner-tubed tires which measured between 4-5 inches wide, mounted on 20-inch wheels. It was difficult to corner because the hard-rubber tires did not have wide tread, thus slippage and lack of traction haunted the drivers. Tire brands in those days were provided by the Firestone, Goodyear and Mason companies and others.

The cars used a mixture of gasoline with tetra-ethyl. The additive benzoil was also used to raise the octane and thus boost the compression ratio.

With the exception of Meyer's Ford, which had cross springs as early as 1924 when the track first opened, suspension for all cars was about the same. The Miller chassis, as the others, used the conventional front and rear side springs. However, when Meyer popped up with cross springs and experienced far better handling (particularly on the high banks), it wasn't long before the cross spring system was installed on a few other cars. (It would be a generation before the invention of torsion bars).

Many of the speed plants had no tails and their rear fuel tanks were clearly visible. Some cars, perhaps stock models which carried two men, even had headlights.

Asked if exposed (unprotected) fuel tanks were dangerous, Meyer said, "A car can burst into flames, with, or without a tail . . . it depends largely how a car is hit."

Meyer (87 years old at this writing) said that the drivers and car builders in those days simply didn't give tails any consideration.

"Heck, the guys installed tails just to pretty them up, I guess . . . streamline them. I don't know, I'm sure they weren't thinking about any safety factor, at least not at the beginning."

Meyer also was the first driver to wheel

a Rajo on the Ascot track. "I was the first man to get a Rajo cylinder head on my Model-T block," he quipped.

The name "Rajo," Meyer said, was taken from the cylinder head's homeplace at Racine, Wisconsin, and from its designer, Joe Jagersburger.

Sixty years ago, and more, California had its share of outstanding race tracks and road courses—the rapid board speedways at Beverly Hills (Los Angeles Speedway), Santa Maria, Fresno and Culver City. Also operating at that time was the Santa Monica Road Race and Corona Road Race, annual events which drew thousands of spectators along city streets and surrounding grandstands, to watch the cloth-helmeted, goggle-eyed speed demons of the day. The mile dirt course at San Luis Obispo was another standout track.

The glorified racing drivers of that period were throttle pushers such as the incomparable Tommy Milton, Leon Duray, Roscoe Sarles, Dario Resta, Jimmy Murphy, DePalma, Eddie Miller, Pete DePaolo, Art Klein, Frank Lockhart, Red Shafer, "Boy Wonder" Harland Fengler, Jim Parsons, Eddie Hearne, Joe Boyer, Jimmy Gleason, Bennett Hill, Ray Keech, Bob McDonough, Bob Burman, Gaston Chevrolet, Harry Hartz, Howard Wilcox and many, many others.

Also operating at that time was the original Ascot auto course, a mile dirt track that was located where today stands the Goodyear Tire & Rubber Company at Central Avenue and Florence Avenue, on the south side of Los Angeles.

As most racing fans know, the first "Ascot" was a horse track in England which still operates today.

Opening in 1912, the original Ascot auto course reaped a financial harvest with promoter George R. Bentel and ace publicity writer William H. Pickens at the helm.

With Pickens grinding out the bally-hoo, he and Bental were able to lure the era's board and dirt track stars on regular basis with big jackpot prizes.

The fans turned out in droves.

Famous motion picture producer Cecil B. DeMille once flew a biplane just above the ground and raced dirt track driver Eddie Hearne in a Duesenberg. Who won the race, though, is lost in time.

Despite its financial success the Ascot mile yielded to urban development and was demolished in 1919. Eventually the colorful board tracks also fell to progress. Records show that the last big board speedway was torn down in 1931 at Altoona, Pennsylvania.

But the name "Ascot" didn't remain dormant long. Bentel and Pickens decided to revive the name and build a new 5/8-mile Ascot after a few years of planning—and dreaming.

Ascot was to find a new home off Valley Boulevard and Soto Street on the outskirts of Alhambra. The year 1924 was to be the start of 13 years of speed, thrills, chills and spills. Thus New Ascot Motor Speedway was born.

Bentel leased thousands of acres from four land holders—the Huntington Land Company, of San Marino, California; the Rohl Manufacturing Company, of Los Angeles; the Jordan Oil Company, also of Los Angeles; and from William May Garland, president of the Los Angeles Athletic Club.

The leased land was partially surrounded by rolling hills overlooking Alhambra. Bulldozers cut into those hills and carved out the beginning stages of what was to be the main auto race track and road course. At first the track was a dust bowl and many helmet-less and goggle-eyed drivers inhaled quite a bit of earth in their brave effort to win at all costs.

Bentel also designed the track and laid

21

out the road course that would be used for the Targo Florio race. Jack Prince, who had built the grandstands at earlier day board speedways, also designed the stands at Ascot. Prince included fancy loge sections for motion picture and sports personalities and other ritzy folk. Despite the lack of top-notch racing equipment at the outset, Bentel and Pickens used their promotional genius to attract large crowds. Featured were "Frontys" and Model-T's, Duesenbergs and other hot jobs.

In its beginning in 1924, Ascot operated without a championship goal for the drivers. Instead, Bentel staged a series of gold cup races each Sunday in addition to other events under Alex Sloane's IMCA sanction. The cash awards appealed to the "name" drivers (DePalma, Lockhart, Frame, Duray, Stapp of the AAA), and the "barnstormers" came from everywhere to drive their dusty tanks and challenge the big shot drivers. The AAA contest board had authorized Bentel to promote "mixed" shows with Sloane.

Actually, Ascot's opening day featured a who's who in auto racing, and the much publicized and record-breaking driver Barney Oldfield spiced many events by serving as referee. The legendary cigar-chomping veteran was respected by all drivers and Ascot track officials.

The first "raw" attraction was DePalma. Later came DePalma's nephew, Peter De-Paolo, who didn't stick around long, instead competed on larger tracks and eventually won the 1925 Indianapolis 500 mile race. After DePaolo emerged Frank Lockhart, a first class driver from Dayton, Ohio. George Souders, a future Indianapolis winner as was Lockhart, was another who received star billing.

However, while DePalma, DePaolo, Lockhart and Souders were enjoying success by trading victories week after week,

another driver had emerged unnoticeably upon the scene. He was Francis Quinn. Although Quinn was not as successful as his four rivals at the beginning, it wasn't long before he matched them victory-for-victory.

Quinn hailed from Washougal, Washington, where he had starred on many dirt tracks between 1919 and 1923. He decided to try his luck in Southern California when he learned that the new Ascot was to open.

Quinn drove the wheels off Cecil Ballanger's "Ballanger Rajo Special" No. 46. It was in this car that he pressed Lockhart, DePalma, Ed Winfield, Leon Duray and the others to the limit.

Quinn was considered an "also-ran" on opening day and for the ensuing nine weeks, but he improved as rapidly as his chariot could spin its wheels and soon started competing for "King of Ascot" laurels.

In those early days the management had erected bleacher-type seating on the north turn hillside in addition to the main stands on the front stretch. The bleachers were in the middle of the turn where many drivers spun out, shot through the fence and struck the bleachers with resounding force. The fans would scatter whenever a roaring racing car came charging their way.

Publicity man Pickens, a great one for Barney Oldfield, for stuntman Lincoln Beachey and for many pioneer auto racers and flyers, cleverly portrayed DePalma as the hero and record-smasher and board track star Leon Duray as the villain of the speedway.

Pickens, using his cunningness, had "hero" DePalma and "bad guy" Duray constantly arguing in the papers before a race.

One of the important promotions of the Bentel-Pickens combine was to be the 200-lap Targo Florio road race which would be staged over two miles of bumpy hills and dusty track in 1925.

Because the track was still rough the cars threw up clouds of dust while they circled the oval and climbed up and down the hills. The race was patterned after the original Targo Florio held years before in Italy. Ascot's race drew thousands of fans who saw "Cannonball" Baker, the bally-hooed "motorcycle and racing car record smasher from coast to coast" snatch a big victory prize. The win was declared official despite protests over a racing technicality filed by Lockhart.

Lockhart was sensational from his very beginning as a racer. He burned up the Ascot course, became the star on the country's board tracks and was the sensation of the Indianapolis time trials of 1926. He had gone to the qualifications only as a mechanic and sightseer. However, he took a ride in Bennett Hill's rapid "Miller Special" (thanks to Frank's long-standing friend and mechanic, Ernie Olson, who was chief mechanic on Hill's car). Lockhart got around the Indy oval faster than everybody, even Hill.

Regular driver Pete Kreis became ill on race day and Lockhart was picked to drive the big Miller. Although heavy rains halted the race at 400 miles, Lockhart was at least five miles ahead at the finish and was crowned champion of the 1926 Memorial Day race. "It was no contest," many a racing fan was heard to say.

Lockhart became the star attraction after DePalma retired from regular Ascot competition. Frank was acclaimed a great mechanic and was one of the most gifted natural drivers ever. In 1928, at age 25, Lockhart was killed when his Stutz Blackhawk experimental car flipped at Daytona Beach at more than 200 miles per hour. Fearless Frank was competing with Ray Keech (who was to win the 1929 Indianapolis race) and with Major H.O.D. Seagrave, whose super huge Sunbeam held the land

speed record. Lockhart lost his life when a rear tire blew on his twin-engine bullet (which he had designed), thus ending his short but spectacular motor racing career. Lockhart was a champion in death—the holder of a new class world speed record.

Duray was an absolutely fearless driver. It was oldtimer Eddie Meyer who said of Duray: "Of all the drivers in history I tip my hat to Leon Duray for his turning Indianapolis at better than 124 miles per hour in 1927. Leon was driving a front-drive Miller . . . a 91 cubic inch job on very narrow tires . . . not like big pillows and the supercharged engines the boys have today. And Leon drove that track when it was all brick, too! That is mighty fast for the equipment that he had. Duray deserves all the credit in the world."

Fred Horey and Sig Haugdahl were imported to beat the fair-haired DePalma. Sig drove his long "Wisconsin Special," but he usually breathed the exhaust fumes of the "Gray Fox."

Eddie Meyer was the diminutive driver from South Gate, by way of Redlands, whose brother Louie was to win the Indianapolis race in 1928, 1933, 1936. Eddie drove a "Riverside Special" No. 6, and also the "Rajo Special" No. 4 Model-T Ford. Eddie many times rode with younger brother Lou at Ascot and on the country's mile tracks. After vacating the speedways Eddie took to boat racing and became one of the nation's foremost boat racers. He competed until he was 62!

Another regular was Eddie Winfield who drove his rapid "Winfield Special" Model-T flathead. (Ed and his brother, Bud Winfield, developed the popular Winfield Carburetor years later).

Pop Evans always drove a hopped-up Model-T with a special Rajo head. Although being much older than the other drivers, even DePalma, Pop competed as often as he could. He became the track's maintenance man after he got too old to race.

Al Hopp, a dirt track racer from nearby Burbank, drove a hopped-up Chevrolet at Ascot. "Fuzzy" Davidson and Jack Petticord tooled Fronty Fords.

New Hampshire's Fred Frame was a great driver and a standout attraction on the eastern boards. Frame competed at Indianapolis for many years and won in 1932. He is also remembered for his duels on the board tracks with Cliff Woodbury and others.

But Ascot's opening day belonged to De-Palma.

DePalma was highly respected, loved and admired. Above all he was a winner on many tracks such as dirt, board, brick, asphalt, cement, and on cross country courses. At one time DePalma even held the land speed record in a Packard. His hard-luck in the 1912 Indianapolis race in which he gallantly tried to push his stalled Mercedes across the finish line after leading the race, only to have Joe Dawson flash to victory, is one of the most memorable and dramatic episodes in racing history.

DePalma's cooperative conduct and sportsmanship earned him the praise of thousands and his friendly manner made it easy for promoters to put his talents to use. But Ralph possessed business acumen as well, and always received top appearance money.

DePalma won at Ascot so often that sometimes suspicion arose that perhaps he was using an illegal motor or supercharger. Inspections were to no avail. It was said that to beat him was a crime. Many tried and almost as many failed. DePalma was always ready to help a fellow driver with a racing part or two, get him in the race, then "Uncle Ralph," as he was affectionately known, would beat him.

DePalma eventually retired and served Ascot Speedway as an official, honarary referee, car sponsor and in various advisory capacities.

DePalma died from natural causes in 1956. He was 73. Up until his end "Uncle Ralph" would visit many tracks and never failed to advise and encourage drivers. The name "DePalma" is legend in auto racing history.

Races continued to be held at the new track throughout February, 1924, under the auspices of Ascot Speedway Association and the IMCA. Financial success was limited.

It was for the March 2 show, however, that the management presented a new printed program, a large brochure, priced at 10 cents, that had names and pictures of drivers and track officials to promote close relations between the drivers and fans.

In charge of track operations were:

Bentel, president; Edgar K. Brown, secretary-treasurer; Pickens, listed as Director of Contests and Exploitations; Frank A. Carbutt, referee in chief; Charlie Keppen, associate referee; Derkum, starter; and Charles H. Branaman, representative of the IMCA.

Judges were J. V. Baldwin, O. Rey Rule, Dwight Whiting, and Dr. James W. White. Technical committeemen were A. C. Webb, Charles Basle, Edward Lingenfelder and veteran racer Eddie Pullen. "Cannonball" Baker was assistant referee. Ambulance service was provided by Ivy Overholtzer, the mortician at nearby White Memorial Hospital in East Los Angeles.

It was Baker who bought the first advertising space in the program, advertising his Nearcar, which, he claimed he drove from New York to Los Angeles for $19.20. The ad read:

"Nearcars average 100 miles per gallon . . . it is the most economical transportation you can buy . . . only $210 here. Cannon-ball Baker & Co., 1016 S. Hill St., Los Angeles."

A house ad labeled, "To Our Patrons," read: "Everything sold in this speedway is 10 cents, except near beer—15 cents. Cigars, cigarettes, tobacco, at city prices. Pay no more. The management will appreciate reporting at the office any discourtesy or overcharge."

The entries for the March 2 race which attracted more than 10,000 spectators were numbered 1 through 51, with the exceptance of Fred Frame's No. 99. They follow:

Sig Haugdahl, Fred Leickleider, Duesenberg Special; Leon Duray, Miller; Sid Chambers, Fram Special; Babe Stapp, Sherman Special; Eddie Meyer, Rajo Special; Fred Luelling, Fronty; Reggie Lyons, Packard; Vic Monks, Strickland Special; Al Melcher, Duesenberg; Fred Horey, Frontenac; Arthur "Fuzzy" Davidson, Fronty; Harold Pimlott, Rajo Special; John Kent, Kent Special, Fred Lyon, Chevrolet Special; Jack Snider, Fresno Special; C. D. (Pop) Evans, Glendale Special ; E.A. (Ed) Winfield, Kant-Score Special; M. Shampang, Chevrolet Special; Eddie Hughes, Florence Special; "Snowy" Browne, Duesenberg; Joe Grijalva, Hudson Special; Chet Carter, Duesenberg; Jack Morris, Whippet Special; Fred Leickleider, Miller Special (listed twice for unknown reason) ; Frank Lockhart, McDowell Special; Robbit Van, Robertson Special; Ernest Wilson, Wilson Special; Jack Cousins, Cousins Special; Lewis Moore, Moore Special (perhaps it was Lou Moore of Indianapolis and Blue Crown Special fame) ; Johnny Vickers, Essex Special; Jack Smith, Fronty; Harold Fredriksen, Cragar; J. T. Jenkins, Duesenberg; Charles Moon, M & M Special; George Miller, Miller Special; Ed Kershaw, Valley Special; "Snapper" Garrison, C & C Special; Fred Horey, (also listed twice)

Frontenac; Tennis Kolts, Hooker Special; Norris Shears, Kings Special; B. W. (Speed) Hinkley, Constantino Special; Floyd Roberts, Grey Essex; D. C. Riner, Delage; Frank Hart, Hart Special; E. R. Jensen, J.M. & S. Special; Gus Shrader, Mais Special; Tennis Kolts (also listed twice) , Monrovia Special; Jack Petticord, Fronty; and Fred Frame, Hooker Special.

Also carded were special motorcycle races that were sanctioned by the Motorcycle and Allied Trades Association, J. J. O'Connor, California Representative. Riders and their mounts were as follows:

Gene Walker, Indian; Ray Weishar, Jim Davis and Ralph Hepburn, Harley-Davidson; Johnny Seymour, Bob Sarkegian, Indians; Glen Stokes, Roy Tweedy, Excelsiors; Blick Walters, C. J. Barrett, Harley-Davidsons; John Duke, Indian; Sam Hamilton, Harley-Davidson.

Duray posted the fastest auto qualifying time of 32.2 seconds, with Frame second and Leickleider, third.

Cyclists were the second event, a one-lap Bentel Helmet Speed 'Em Up Motorcycle Contest. Seymour was first, followed by Walker. From a flying start Seymour won in 32 seconds. Seymour snatched the helmet previously won by Jim Davis, thus keeping it until he lost it, Johnny also got a fifty dollar prize for each week that he kept the crown.

Race cars came back for the third event, a one-lap dash for the Ascot Helmet. Duray beat all rivals, followed by Leickleider, Eddie Meyer and Frame in that order.

"Fuzzy" Davidson won the 10-lap invitational, with E. R. Jensen second.

The cycles came roaring back for the Paul Derkum Stakes five lapper. Walker beat Kreiger as each bike broadslided through the dusty turns.

Race cars were featured in the sixth race . . . the Edwin Hubbell Stakes 20-lap main.

Eddie Meyer fought off Frame and **Babe** Stapp in a cloud of dust.

It was in this race that Ascot claimed its first two victims. Driver Norris Shears and riding mechanic Jimmy Craft spun on the back straightaway in the "Kings Special" Fronty Ford. The double-seater slammed against the fence and bounced crazily back onto the track spewing oil all over the surface. Shears was killed instantly and Craft died hours later. The car's entire front end was demolished.

Event No. 7 was the "Cannonball" Baker Handicap for cycles. Seymour won the 10 lapper. Walker and Kreiger were second and third.

Barnstorming driver Sig Haugdahl was the feature star in event No. 8. Sig was listed as "driving one lap exhibitions with his 'Wonder Car,' which he made the world's record of 180 miles per hour at Daytona Beach, Florida." Sig was timed in 30 seconds flat as he displayed his powerful "Wisconsin Special."

Event No. 9, the 10-lap Quadrangular Championship Match for race cars wound up the show. Haugdahl, driving a Fiat, threw up the dust and won by the margin of a radiator shell over Leickleider and Eddie Meyer.

Perhaps the death of Shears symbolized the danger that was to become associated with Ascot history, for more fatalities were to occur on its high banks and speedpaths.

"Fellas, the track's all yours," would be the appropriate thought to enter starter Fred "Pop" Wagner's mind, as he waved the starting flag at Mel Kenealy, on pole, and Clarence Downing in the "Kleopfer Special" No. 33 on the outside. In the second row on the outside is Bill "Red" Heisler. Driver of the "hog" on the inside is unidentified. The day is September 27, 1929, at the Legion Ascot Speedway.

Racing great "Cannonball" Baker who competed in Ascot's first race in 1924. Baker was also a motorcycle racer "from coast to coast" and was highly regarded among barnstorming and pioneer racing drivers at the turn of the century.

View of Targo Florio road race course in 1925. Driver is unidentified. Note headlamps on two-man racing car.
(Courtesy Roscoe Turner.)

Barnstorming drivers get "feel" of the rough dirt surface in 1924. Who are they? Does anybody know? (Note livestock outside north turn). Animals and trees were removed to install stretch of bleachers. The bleachers were removed in 1927, thereafter the area declared out of bounds because of extreme danger caused by accelerating racing cars.
(Courtesy Roscoe Turner.)

"Cannonball" Baker sees if Ascot's early day dirt surface is to his liking as he prepares for the 1924 Gold Cup race. He's driving a Jewett, and carrying license plates, too! (Courtesy Roscoe Turner.)

"Cannonball" Baker, takes a practice spin in his Jewett on Ascot's Targo Florio road course in 1925. The hillside course was especially laid out for the big event which drew drivers from throughout the country. The race, which attracted thousands of spectators, was won by Frank Lockhart.
(Alvarez-Craig.)

Cars! Cars! Cars! Lined up and ready for a 1926 gold cup race at the refined Ascot track. Note the grandstand constructed outside the north turn. "Cannonball" Baker's Jewett No. 1 is at extreme right. (Doug Boyd collection.)

Warm 'em up and let 'em go. Scene is the starting line of the Gold Cup race of 1924. Two-man and single seat racers were used that year, as depicted. (Alvarez-Craig.)

Cars zoom out of the north turn to receive the starting flag during a 1927 race. Bleachers on hillside were installed in 1926 and were removed a year later because of danger to the spectators. Only the main grandstand on the home stretch would remain until the track's demise in 1936. (Alvarez-Craig.)

Before a near-capacity crowd at old Ascot, the drivers line up four abreast for a gold cup event about 1926. On the pole is a Hudson No. 21 driven by Floyd Roberts. No. 27 is Ray Mcdowell's. No. 27 SR Fronty single overhead cam driven by Frank Lockhart. In Car No. 30 is Jim Reed in the "Morasco Special". Lockhart was 1926 Indy champ; Roberts won in 1938. (Doug Boyd collection.)

Targo Florio road race, 1925. A splendid candid shot of the road course, front straightaway and infield parking for cars and fans. Note hundreds of spectators on hillsides.. (Alvarez-Craig.)

This 1932 photo shows Ralph DePalma standing beside his "Miller Special" in which Mrs. DePalma is seated. The great champion, a credit to racing the world, drove his car many times at Ascot.

The great Ralph De Palma in his famous No. 1 Miller at Ascot on December 13, 1930. Despite 23 years behind the wheel of a racing car, the 1915 Indianapolis champ gave his much younger adversaries a tough time of it.

Ralph De Palma was a gentleman off the track and a great driver on one. He was known to furnish many drivers race car parts, then beat them! Here's "Uncle Ralph" on January 13, 1928, at Ascot, the year the American Legion entered the promotional picture.

The legendary Ralph De Palma, Ascot Speedway, 1926. This historical picture shows De Palma receiving Victory Crown helmet which was created in his honor by the Vai brothers of Cucamonga, California. De Palma, 1915 Indianapolis winner, won the helmet 7 times at Ascot.

Young Frank Lockhart (22 years old) thunders down the Ascot hillside on way to winning the 1925 Thankgiving Day Gold Cup race over the dangerous dirt course. Lockhart is seen broad-sliding into the lead on his way to victory.

Ascot was a dirt track in this 1927 photo. A year later road oil would be applied, making the dirt-oil surface smooth and considerably faster. Note cabled fencing on the inside of the north turn, a perilous condition non-existent today. Does anybody recognize these speedsters? (Courtesy Roscoe Turner.)

Action at Ascot Speedway in 1926. In lead is Ralph DePalma in his No. 1 "Miller Special." Second is Fred Horey in his No. 11 Fronty Ford. Fred Leickleider drives the No. 28 Duesenberg. Eddie Meyer tools the No. 6 "Riverside Special" Model-T.

"Fuzzy" Davidson, famed dirt track driver of the 1920's, is shown on opening day at Ascot, 1924. Davidson, Ralph DePalma, Eddie Meyer, Fred Horey, "Cannonball" Baker and Fred Leicklider, among others, thrilled the crowd during the curtain raiser.

Fred Merzney, veteran southwestern states and Ascot Speedway driver.

Fred Leickleider, who drove in Ascot's first race in 1924.

Veteran race starter Fred "Pop" Wagner flanked by Ralph De Palma, right, and Norman Manning, AAA official at Ascot on January 26, 1928. It was the start of the 1928 season and all was aglow on the newly paved 5/8-mile track.

The highly respected, Dr. Fred W. Loring, head of the Race Board of American Legion Post 127, Glendale, California. It was Dr. Loring's group which helped put Ascot on the racing map in 1928. He died November 15, 1975.

(Courtesy Roscoe Turner.)

Fred "Pop" Wagner, the most famous race starter in the sport's history. Wagner started many races on many U.S. tracks since 1902, including the famous board speedways of the 1920s. Wagner died in 1933.

"I gave Louie his first ride," said Eddie Meyer, behind the wheel of the "Rajo Special" in 1924. Seated beside his older brother is Louie Meyer. The car had top speed of 120 mph. Louie won the Indianapolis Speedway race in 1928-33-36. Eddie later became a famous speedboat racer. (Courtesy Roscoe Turner.)

Tony Morasco in his "Morasco Special" Model-T about 1925. No protection for the driver in those days . . . 85 miles per hour on the straightaways, too! Note exposed gasoline tank behind the driver.

Dirt track demon Ralph Ormsby in his Fronty Ford, Ascot Speedway, August 17, 1924. (Directly behind Ormsby in Arthur Chevrolet, noted racing car builder, owner, promoter, and developer of Chevrolet auto.)

Eddie Meyer drove in Ascot's first race in 1924 and later became an outstanding speedboat racer. He is Louie's big brother (or should we say "little?"). Eddie introduced cross-spring suspension at Ascot.

Driver Bud Hyatt ready to qualify for December 8, 1927 race at Ascot. Car owner-builder Cecil Ballanger stands at right.

Lloyd Axel in Vic Felt's "Felt Special." Vic was unable to drive that night so Lloyd got behind the wheel and qualified for the evening's main event. The year: July 15, 1931.

"Pop" Evans sits proudly in the Model-T "Glendale Special" in 1924. Evans was caretaker of the Ascot track after he retired from competition.

Barney Kloepfer and his rapid Fronty Ford "Barney Special" in 1925. Kloepfer hailed from the Banning area, where he raced before making his invasion of Ascot. (Courtesy Joe Crocker.)

Veteran Fred Horey in his Frontenac speedster, 1924. When the dust blew, and cleared, old Fred was usually up front with the leaders.

Al Hopp, ready for action in his "Chevrolet Special." Hopp was from Burbank, California. The car is tailless and its frame is strapped to the front axle to control vibration. In car No. 16 is Herman Schurch, who was killed at Ascot in 1931. This ready-for-action picture was taken on March 21, 1925.

Dino Massenelli seated in a 1924 Ascot Speedway racing car.

Francis Quinn in 1925 when he drove Cecil Ballanger's No. 46 "Ballanger Special" Fronty Ford during his early days at Ascot. One of the most popular drivers ever to drive at the track, Quinn died in an unfortunate highway accident in 1931.

Francis Quinn in the "Ballanger Rajo" in 1925. Quinn, the "Bald Eagle," drove at Ascot the year the track was opened. He became a standout driver and won Pacific Southwest laurels in 1930. Cecil Ballanger was owner of this car. (Note leather strap tied from frame to front axle, a method of reducing vibration in those days. Similar strap is at rear of car.)

In February 1924, Ascot experienced its first fatal wreck in crash of the "King's Special" which resulted in two deaths. The double-seat Fronty Ford slammed into the fence coming out of the south turn, killing driver Norris Shears and riding mechanic Jimmy Craft.

Jimmy Craft, victim in Ascot's first fatality in 1924. Craft was riding mechanic for driver Norris Shears who was also killed.

Frank Lockhart was acclaimed one of the most gifted and natural drivers in the history of auto racing. The 1926 Indianapolis winner drove this car at Ascot and on board speedways. Lockhart possessed rare engineering talent until his untimely death at Daytona Beach, Florida, in 1928, in the experimental "Stutz Blackhawk," in which he tried for a land speed record. (Doug Boyd collection.)

The incomparable Frank Lockhart started his electrifying racing and engineering career at Ascot and won the 1926 Indianapolis race. Lockhart, a sensation on America's board tracks as well, won the big Targo Florio event in 1925. He was killed in a speed test in 1928 at Daytona Beach, Florida. Lockhart was photographed on August 24, 1925.

Frank Lockhart in Ray McDowell's "McDowell's Special" in what perhaps was Ascot's first night racing event. The year is 1925. Ascot introduced night racing on regular basis in 1927. Four abreast start in those days; Lockhart's car is an SR Fronty SOC (single overhead cam job.)

(Doug Boyd collection.)

Action on Ascot's dusty dirt track as the cars zoom out of the north turn. The day is July 4, 1927. Herman Schurch (16) and unidentified drivers pour it on.

Ascot action in 1927. Note tailess race car with fuel tank at rear and battery lying alongside frame. Driver on left appears more "up-dated," in that his car has a tail. The unidentified drivers (who are they?) lean to left as they steam into the south turn.   (Courtesy Roscoe Turner)

Motorcycle racing was a very popular sport at Ascot during the 1920s. Note huge crowd on hillside overlooking north turn. Just as many crowd the infield parking area. Action, January 21 1927. Rajo sign on hillside appropriately advertises the noted Rajo racing equipment.

F.W. (Fred) Bobzein, prominent Eastern driver who successfully invaded Pacific Southwest tracks, including Ascot, in 1926. His car is one typical of the Fronty Fords driven by drivers of the day.

(Courtesy Joe Crocker.)

Dirt track driver "Snapper" Garrison behind the wheel of a typical two-seat racer that was in competition at Ascot during the early 1920s.

(left) Efrieda (Frieda Maes, famous woman racing driver of the 1920s. Pictured at Ascot on April 25, 1926. Frieda was one of the first woman racers and an IMCA (International Motor Contest Association) barnstorming driver. This very unique racing machine is an Essex.

Over and down hills, under bridges, around the track and what have you. That was the Ascot scene during the 1925 Thanksgiving Day Gold Cup race won by Frank Lockhart. It was a gruelling grind of 100 laps over the hilly dirt course. "Cannonball" Baker filed a protest, but it was to no avail as Lockhart was awarded victory.

Dead-panned Fred Horey actually used to grimace while fighting for the lead as the dust flew during Ascot's early days. This is Fred in his primitive days as a racing driver on March 5, 1918!

Sig Haugdahl was known as a famous barnstorming driver from coast-to-coast. Sig competed in the 1925 Targo Florio road race. Aerial stuntman Lincoln Beachey was Haugdahl's barnstorming buddie.

A man of many racing missions . . . that was Babe Stapp. He missed Ascot's opening day event due to mechanical trouble. Stapp became a standout attraction, however. Babe was Midwest champ and also drove in 13 Indianapolis races.

Leon Duray was known as the "villian of Ascot." Oldtimers vow that Duray's 124 mph lap average in a Miller front drive at Indianapolis in 1927, is the most courageous driving performance in the history of auto racing.

Noel Bullock, of Banning, California, drove many cars and built as many for Ascot speed demons.

Harlan Fengler, the "Boy Wonder" of board speedway racing in 1924 at the Culver City board track. Fengler promoted races at Ascot in 1926-27, later became chief steward at Indianapolis Speedway.

Charley Gelston, prominent driver at Ascot Speedway. Gelston was among the top ranking drivers during the 1926-29 seasons.

Fred Frame of New Hampshire as he appeared at Ascot in 1924. Drivers wore only caps and goggles during those dust flying days. Frame won the 1932 Indianapolis 500.

CHAPTER II

THE FIRST CHAMPIONS

(1926 - 1928)

Oldtimers Bid Adieu

Promotional Problems

Mechanical Deficiencies

Young Speed Demons

Buxton Wins, Retires

Pillsbury Stresses Safety

Ascot Developments

Mel Kenealy, 1929 Champ

Movie Stars Abound

Dr. Loring's Legionnaires

Death Takes No Holiday

With aging Ralph DePalma retired from Ascot competition in the 1920s (he quit racing altogether in 1935), races continued to be furiously contested and the track steadily became the most dangerous speedway in the annals of motor racing.

While the retired DePalma assisted Ascot as an official or honorary referee, New Hampshire's Fred Frame also departed Ascot action by 1926 in favor of eastern tracks. Sig Hougdahl and his famed "Wisconsin Special," "Fuzzy" Davidson, "Pop" Evans and "Cannonball" Baker had also joined the retired list. Evans assumed the track's caretakership for Bentel-Pickens promotions.

The great Frank Lockhart, like DePalma, also vacated Ascot, choosing to concentrate on the AAA's huge, high-banked board speedways on which he was to set many records. Frank's meteoric career was cut short in 1928, however, in the fatal accident at Daytona Beach, Florida.

Babe Stapp chose Ascot over his native Texas as his "second home." It was in 1927 when Stapp began his 13 tries at winning the Indianapolis Speedway race. Between races at Ascot, Stapp burned up the Eastern AAA circuit and was crowned Midwest AAA champion one year.

Ed Winfield put his rapid "Winfield Special" supercharged Model-T flathead in mothballs and went into business with younger brother, Bud, to improve their popular and efficient downdraft carburetor.

Eddie Meyer also quit Ascot and chose to build racing cars and operate a South Gate automotive garage. But whenever Eddie was bitten by the "racing bug" he'd ride with younger brother Louie as a mechanic on the mile tracks of the National AAA circuit.

Leon Duray remained at Ascot and resumed his role as "villain" to arouse and heckle the drivers who were receiving fea-

ture star billing. Duray also continued his breathtaking exploits at Indianapolis and on the rapid board tracks.

Although Ascot operated with reasonable success from 1924, it found itself in 1927 without a promoter. Founder-owner George Bentel, realizing that attendance was sagging, decided to entertain other promotional ventures (outside of racing) and took with him publicity writer Pickens. But Pickens, stating he missed the excitement of the roaring road, returned a few weeks later to resume his bally-hoo stunts under the promotions of Bon McDoughall and Harry Lutz. (It is believed, as stated by oldtimers in years gone by, that Bentel had departed due to IRS intervention regarding some back taxes).

Despite Pickens' publicity stunts Ascot attendance continued to wane under McDoughall and Lutz who had taken over the promotions in February, 1927. The McDoughall-Lutz setup lasted but six months when low attendance made it impossible to continue promotions. (Oldtimers today also make reference to "rubber checks" left floating around by the promoters).

Lutz called it quits and McDoughall, going it alone, tried to increase attendance but experienced little success.

Meanwhile, a world's title boxing match was to be promoted on the speedway grounds. Dick Donald, a Los Angeles boxing promoter, matched flyweight champion Frankie Genaro of New York, against Los Angeles product Fidel LaBarba, a transplanted New Yorker, who today makes his home in the Southland. Donald rigged up a ring on the main straightaway and also installed hundreds of seats around the ring. The 15-round title bout attracted thousands who saw LaBarba punch out a unanimous decision and win the 112-pound crown as his manager George Blake leaped into the ring hysterically. There were no knockdowns during the rapid war between the two little men.

After the last blow had landed, Ascot closed its doors to racing and remained idle for six months. McDoughall, as did Lutz, bade adieu to Ascot racing promotions.

Harland Fengler, "Boy Wonder" of board track racing who carved himself a famous name on many other tracks and who years later became chief steward at Indianapolis Motor Speedway, took over Ascot in August 1927. Fengler, who obtained AAA sanction for Ascot Speedway, was more successful than Lutz or McDoughall but he didn't remain very long.

During the McDoughall regime Ascot had been invaded by a host of young speed-thirsty racing drivers, many of whom were to become stars. Among the invaders were San Diego's Jack Buxton and Mel Kenealy, a World War I Navy veteran. At this time not only were victories at Ascot necessary to win the Pacific Southwest crown but wins also were required at Bakersfield, Phoenix and El Centro, California, mile ovals and at Banning and Tucson, Arizona, and at San Jose, which were 5/8th mile ovals like Ascot.

Since Ascot was the most appealing because of year-round races, the Pacific Southwest title was habitually nicknamed "Ascot title." To Ascot fans the other tracks held little importance in the championship circuit because they believed Ascot was "it" in competition.

Besides Buxton and Kenealy other throttle stompers who invaded Ascot in 1927 were Charley Gelston, Bill Spence, Bill Bundy, Arvol Brunmier, lanky Ernie Triplett, Walt May, Jimmy Sharp, Kelly Petillo (who was to win the Indianapolis 500 in 1935), Al Gordon, Stubby Stubblefield (who was killed in the 1935 Indianapolis time trials), and many others. These newcomers had joined Francis Quinn, George Souders and other veterans who had raced in Ascot's inaugural program in 1924.

Triplett was a motorcycle racer and bike race enthusiast from Paris, Illinois, but Ernie soon turned to race cars because their competition offered more "gold" than the two-wheelers. Blond Ernie, an intrepid man, was to become known as the "Blond Terror" and the "Belvedere Badboy" at Ascot.

Al Gordon was a mail carrier from Redlands, California, who had been bitten by the "speed bug" about 1925 when he drove Eddie Meyer's Model-T at Banning Speedway. "I gave Al his first ride in my wooden spoke wheeled speed job," Meyer related.

Stubblefield, whose bright smile revealed a front gold tooth, was an iron-fisted driver with a strong will to win. "Stubby," Sharp, Quinn, Petillo, Walt May and Brunmier—great friends off the track—were bitter enemies on it. Petillo, a Huntington Park vegetable truck driver, achieved the highest acclaim of this awesome bunch of leadfoots—his 1935 Indy win.

Ascot's major competition centered around these young daredevils who took unbelievable risks on the track's dangerous high banks and rapid straightaways in daring efforts to earn a racing reputation. They were constantly involved in nerve-wracking racing which would leave the fans limp from excitement and sometimes in sorrow—because of a smashup.

With AAA sanction at Ascot and with the departure of unsuccessful promoters such as Lutz, McDoughall and Fengler, it was Art Pillsbury who took over the operations of the speedway. Pillsbury not only was the Western Region director of the AAA Contest Board but had also designed many board track speedways.

Pillsbury installed new guardrails and other safety features at Ascot but even these precautions didn't deter the death toll.

Brave men unfortunately sacrificed their lives while racing there to gain a springboard to the big apple—Indianapolis.

Ascot, with the younger drivers fighting off each other at dizzy speeds, was beginning to gain national acclaim. Steady work on the track and application of oil on the dirt surface made Ascot smooth as main street and fast.

Ascot's historical "firsts" included:

• Inaugurated night racing on a regular basis in 1927;

• Was the first track to feature the Vai Brothers Victory Crown;

• Was the first American track where a crash helmet was to be first worn in competition (Wilbur Shaw, 1932);

• First track that would present Best Appearing Car and Crew cash awards;

• Would establish the point system which is used today;

• First track to install separate car pits with corresponding race car numbers on the pit wall (for car-pit identification purposes);

• First track that would hold match races on a regular schedule;

• Inaugurated the "Helmet Dash" featuring the two fastest qualifying cars in a special three-lap race (known today as the Trophy Dash);

• First track that would establish Class B championship point standings;

• Where the first photo cell timer was used in a sporting event. Racing cars were previously timed with piano wire strung across the track. Harrald Harper, of Colton, California, developed the photo cell timer in 1930.

Not only was Ascot first in these categories but the steady attendance of movie stars from nearby Hollywood filmland gave the track an enormous appeal and instilled a glamorous atmosphere. They also induced the management to make the track a setting for filming many automobile racing motion pictures.

Among the first movie stars to attend the races were Charlie Chaplin, Loretta Young, William Powell, Douglas Fairbanks, Sr., Mary Pickford, Jack Oakie, Constance Bennett, Wallace Beery, "It Girl" Clara Bow, June Knight, Edward G. Robinson, Bing Crosby, Vince Barnett, silent star Lew Cody, Clark Gable and many others. The populace gleamed with enthusiasm—and thrills. The hoi ploi, meanwhile, could rub elbows with these film personalities.

The introduction of night racing appealed to the thousands of fans. Unfortunately, however, night racing did not exclude the possibility of death on the track. It was on June 29, 1927, the first night program, when Ascot claimed another life . . . in fact, two lives.

Drivers Nick Guglielmi and Jack Petticord were engaged in a furious battle for first place during a 15-lap consolation race when the pair was involved in a wreck near the grandstand along the main straightaway and literally ran down a group of men standing alongside the track near the starting line. Guglielmi was killed instantly as was police official J. D. Cornwall, who had been standing with the group. Petticord was seriously injured as were others near the starting line. Nick Martino went on to win the first-ever night main event, a 75 lapper.

Despite the toll of lives on Ascot's perilous speedpaths (the dangerous south turn was to become known as "King of the Grim Reapers"), Pillsbury was determined and strived for higher payoffs for the drivers.

Ascot maintained its original 5/8th's mile size throughout its existence. It also became one of the fastest tracks in the country because 65 per cent of the course was taken up in wide and banked turns. Oldtimers will say that Ascot ranked unmatched in

49

competition in its overall history. Wilbur Shaw supported this opinion when the diminutive driver from the midwest (he was to win Indianapolis in 1937-39-40) was quoted, "To win the Pacific Southwest Championship at Ascot is tougher than the National title because the competition is so fierce. Never in my racing days had I seen anything like this."

One of the last big time drivers to depart Ascot was George Souders, who won the 1927 Indianapolis race. Souders' departure to compete only on larger tracks apparently inspired younger drivers to invade Ascot.

Bert Spencer of Redlands, California, was one of them. Spencer burned up New Mexico tracks and was to win Ascot's first 100 lap race on September 28, 1927, in his "Redlands Special" No. 6.

Like Spencer, most of the drivers tooled "Fronty" Fords. Very few could afford expensive Miller motor speedsters that were designed by their famous creator Harry Miller.

Francis Quinn was among the "poor" racers who drove a "Fronty." His was the "Ballanger Rajo" owed by Cecil Ballanger of Glendale, California. At this time Quinn was a busy car builder. He had built the "Schmidt Special," a car with a 91 cubic inch Miller Motor which he drove successfully. Also on the planning board was his "Dayton Thorobred Special" in which also he'd install a Miller motor.

Other "Fronty" drivers at this time were Triplett in Barney Kleopfer's "Barney Special" No. 33, Bill Bundy in his "Dizzy 100 Special," Walt May in the "Multi-Ford Special," Jack Buxton, who would switch from the "Par Special" to the "Bobby Special." Mel Kenealy was one of the few younger drivers who avoided "Fronty" Fords and chose to drive Harry Hooker's

"Hooker Special" No. 99 supercharged Model-T.

But somehow, "Whittier Shiek" Arvol Brunmier obtained a Miller racing car and the mustachoed speedster was considered "top stuff" during those unpredictable days. Brunmier's car was the "Piston Ring Shop Special" No. 48 and was powered by a four-cylinder Miller Marine motor.

The 1927 racing season ended with Ascot's younger crop of Quinn, Brunmier, May, Stubblefield, Bundy, Spence, Jimmy Sharp, Spencer and the others breaking necks to earn a "racing reputation."

Pillsbury opened the 1928 season in January by staging a 100 lap main event. Bundy, driving like a madman, overcame almost "impossible odds" (according to the press releases) and won the main event before a capacity crowd. The "impossible odds" were due to the fact that Bundy had spun his "Dizzy" four places, and sped on to victory!

It was later in the 1928 season when the Ascot "death gong" rang once again. Another driver "made" the list of Ivy Overholtzer, the undertaker at nearby White Memorial Hospital who had an agreement with the track—to provide a place to take its dead.

On the night of Aug. 4, 1928, Dud Ludwig took one chance too many and shot out of control while coming out of the north turn, slammed into the fence with tremendous force and flipped several times like a car caught in a twister. Ludwig never regained consciousness. Early reports, though never substantiated, attributed the death to heart failure.

Despite the sudden appearance of the Grim Reaper once again, Ascot's fearless drivers continued to burn up the smokepaths in their race to glory—or death.

Although DePalma had surrendered the red-hot competition to the young "invaders", the Italian ace's coveted Italian Victory Crown remained at the track as an inspiration for the drivers in future "Helmet Dashes."

Spence and Kenealy won the dash repeatedly with Quinn, Charley Gelston and Triplett also winning a share. It was Jack Buxton, though, who amassed the most seasonal points for his numerous main event wins and was crowned Pacific Southwest champion for 1928. Gelston finished a close second, followed by Triplett, Spence, and Quinn. At the tail-end of the standings was Earl Hovenden who had experienced plenty of bugs in his "Fronty" throughout the season.

After he had won the 1928 Southwest title, Buxton retired. But the tall, trim and mustachoed racer had other talents. He became Ascot's staff artist as a sideline to other business ventures. Buxton's "big head" sketches of fellow drivers appeared weekly in book-thick programs which sold for 15 cents. The drawings resembled the drivers perfectly and are collector's items today.

The 1920s period of racing at Ascot was approaching its end and many cars were still tail-less and carried their fuel tanks or oil tanks visibly at the rear or side of the body . . . remaining unprotected from impact. Other cars had their bodies secured to their frames with leather straps at the front and rear axles. The idea was to minimize vibrations and for better handling. Despite these hazardous and primitive conditions the "Frontys" and Millers were "hitting" 90 mph on the straights, with tires only the width of motorcycle tires. Blowouts were imminent with eerie results. A driver remained unprotected, so to speak, unless he ducked under the cowl during a crash . . . that's if he was small enough to crawl under and push up on the steering wheel to brace himself.

Buxton and the other drivers turned Ascot's 5/8th's mile in 29-30 seconds, a respectable speed for the canvas-helmeted phenoms, considering that the rail-framed racers were hard to handle on the treacherous surface. Once a car went out of control on the "marbles" high on a turn, somersaulting over the fence (the south turn in this case) and plunging down the deep embankment was a certainty.

The drivers had lowered by two seconds the previous speed marks of Frame, Baker and Lockhart. Quinn snapped DePalma's Ascot record of 29.04 with a 28 seconds flat in 1928.

It was in early October, 1928, when only five racing programs remained in the season and all drivers were automatically eliminated from the championship by Buxton's big point lead, that Ascot took another turn with the American Legion Post 127, of Glendale, California.

Dr. Fred W. Loring, a mild-mannered dentist, worked with Pillsbury to put Ascot on the high plane of motor racing.

The Legion, with Dr. Loring calling the shots and with Pillsbury's expertise, took over the Ascot promotions. One of the Legion's first acts was to add its name to the speedway's title and thus AMERICAN LEGION SPEEDWAY was born.

Dr. Loring described the Legion takeover:

"Kenny Paine, our commander of Post 127, had requested that I assume chairmanship of a Boy Scout committee. Seems the Legion wanted to participate in a community program . . . but the Boy Scout program was not my forte.

"We had also been advised that Ascot was having financial and promotional difficulties and Post 127 had been asked by the AAA to assist in promoting the track . . . under AAA sanction, of course.

"I was told that other promoters had

51

lost money, that (Harlan) Fengler also had departed as promoter, leaving the opportunity open to the Legion. The Post contacted Mr. Pillsbury, regional director of the AAA, and arrangements were made to have Post 127 assume the promotions. The venture excited me and I decided to give the challenge my best effort. We just got in there and gambled."

With Paine as post commander and Dr. Loring heading the Contest Board, the Legion's Glen Mapes took charge of concessions and Harry Schmidt was named plant superintendent. Old driver "Pop" Evans handled track maintenance. Other legionnaires participating in the promotions were W. King Provan, Gene Gilliland, Henry Prussing, John Lichtig. Edgar Johnson, W. H. "Reg" Regelin, Robert Rowley, Walter Richards and others.

Bill Pickens remained in charge of publicity, Herb Marow handled the radio commentary over Station KHJ and Regelin was public address announcer, besides providing printed programs and sales.

For the AAA, Pillsbury installed George Stephenson as chairman of the Technical Committee, Fred Betz was chief timer, veteran Fred "Pop" Wagner was named chief starter. Wagner had been in racing since 1903. Bill Claus became pit manager, Bill Koller was assistant starter under Wagner, and legendary Barney Oldfield was referee.

Dr. Loring and Pillsbury presided over everything, and anybody. Pillsbury arranged races as regional director for the AAA Contest Board and the Legion promoted, promoted, promoted. Everything started to jell for American Legion Speedway.

It was on Thanksgiving Day 1928, when the Legion promoted its first race—a 100 lap main event which was won by Mel Kenealy, with Francis Quinn finishing second, inches behind the high-flying Irishman's "Hooker Special" No. 99. A screaming crowd of more than 10,000 watched enthusiastically.

The Legion kept promoting the track and its drivers. Legionnaires would post signboards, tack up posters by the hundreds throughout Los Angeles. Others maintained track security, some took charge of parking, huge newspaper ads were bought to publicize events and the name "Ascot" was heard over the radio. The Legion also paid for mounted police who kept the fans out of the north turn hillsides and other danger areas. Legionnaires also served as ticket takers, ushers, door keepers and caretakers of the vast auto parking areas. They were paid $4 per day for their services. No doubt the uniformed Legionnaires added class to the Ascot scene.

Wrestling promoter Lou Darrow of the Los Angeles Olympic Auditorium, offered advice on publicity and also suggested night racing each Wednesday.

Dr. Loring and his Legion assistants arranged to have movie starlets present trophies and the Victory Crown Helmet to winning drivers to spice up the show. The idea had terrific impact on the populace. Stars such as Loretta Young, Genevieve Tobin, Constance Cummings, Sally Blaine, Constance Bennett, June Knight, Peggy Hamilton, Celeste Edwards, Jeanne Dunn, Gilda Grey and many others, did their "thing"—plant a kiss on the triumphant driver.

The track steamrolled into financial success and the repercussion was felt throughout the racing world. With the exception of Indianapolis Motor Speedway, Ascot became the most famous and most populated race course in the country.

Dr. Loring stated briefly:

"The track lost money under previous promoters . . . under the Legion the track made money immediately . . . our financial gains increased season by season. We did pretty well. We made more than $60,000 clear profit one year . . . I can't recall what year it was," said the aging man.

Dr. Loring also brought in the Post 127 American Legion Band which helped spice many a program. Under the direction of Bandmaster George Kryder the band played every Wednesday night and Sunday afternoon. Heard were tunes such as the Artillery March, "Betty Coed," and "Ninety-Nine Out of a Hundred Kiss in the Dark, Why Don't You?", among other lively favorites of the time.

Dr. Loring added, "Our objective was to bring a good racing attraction to the fans . . . by the best drivers . . . the best racing cars. We had good, clean thoughts all the way around. This was the Post's first venture into auto racing and it was thrilling."

As for the drivers, Dr. Loring had kind words for them as well:

"Racing drivers are a great bunch . . . a strange breed. They are very sincere . . . all on the up and up. There's nothing phoney about the racing driver. It's a gutty business. It can't be phoney if he's going to be out there risking his life."

Legion Post 127 maintained offices in the Arcade Building, Fourth and Spring streets, Los Angeles. Meetings were held there specifically for Ascot promotions. Large pictures of racing cars and drivers were posted throughout the corridors.

Plant superintendent Harry Schmidt said that Ascot was strictly a dirt track with a slight coating of oil when the Legion took over in 1928. "We would apply new coatings of heavy, thick, crude oil . . . we'd add gravel and work the oil into the surface with rollers each week, or whenever it was necessary."

He added, "We tried to make the track as fast as possible . . . and maintain safety standards as well. But it became very dangerous with speeds going up . . . human error . . . defective equipment." Schmidt cited faulty steering mechanisms, bad wheel spindles, tires blowing out and faulty tie rods as the real menace to the nervy drivers. "I'd say that exposed gasoline tanks were dangerous but one of the lesser dangers. The big problem was the unbelievable chances the drivers were taking. How can you tell a racing driver to slow down?" Schmidt offered.

Attendance continued on the upswing. Triplett, Quinn, Walt May, Bill Spence, Phil Pardee, Bill Bundy, Kenealy, Ralph Ormsby and his "Fronty Special," Ted Simpson and his big 12 cylinder Chrysler and Kenny Stoddard burned up the track to the delight of the speed crazed fans. Lou Moore, who arrived in 1927, was another leadfoot in competition. Moore was to gain fame years later with his "Blue Crown Specials" at Indianapolis Speedway.

Not long after the Legion takeover tragedy struck again. Likeable Kenny Stoddard crashed to his death on Dec. 22, 1928, when he tried to pass two cars on the fatal south turn but lost control, went into a crazy spin, plunged against the fence, rolled several times and came to rest in an upright position. The stands screamed, then quieted. A billow of smoke was seen emitting from the wreckage on the south turn where the racer came to a halt. Ascot had claimed another victim.

With the Legion in high gear the drivers began to get more pay. Many got rides in "class" cars. One was the "Padre Special," a 191 cubic inch Miller which was owned by the Vai Brothers of Cucamonga, the same family who had brought the Victory Crown Helmet to honor DePalma. Kenealy drove the Miller at dizzy speeds.

The slender Kenealy had driven the

"Hooker Special" No. 99, but switched to the lighter and more rapid "Padre" midway in the 1929 season. In this car he would zoom to the Southwest crown that year.

The point standings as of June 15, 1929, read:

Kenealy, 113.93; Triplett, 97.72; Bill Spence, 61.67 (in memorium; he was killed in the 1929 Indianapolis race); Walt May, 46.65; Bill Heisler, 45.46; Jimmy Sharp, 41.17; Johnny Sawyer, 36.51; Phil Pardee, 36.30; Woody Woodford, 34.81; Francis Quinn, 25.40; Babe Stapp, 3.00; and down to Clarence Downing, 2.00.

The point standings as of June 24, 1929, were:

Kenealy 136.81; Triplett, 97.72; Spence (in memorium, 61.67); Jimmy Sharp, 55.08; Walt May, 53.49; Bill Heisler, 53.24; Speed Hinkley, 44.19; Quinn, 42.83; Nick Martino, 40.31; and down to Charley Robertson, 0.63.

The Champion Sparkplug Trophy went to car No. 3, owned by Thomas Mahoney, for the car that made the best all-around appearance. Runner-up was Russ Garnant's car No. 18. Others were R. C. Schwerin, car No. 55; Eddie Gates, car No. 43; and Guy Deulen, car No. 91.

Pillsbury remained as AAA regional director, but Theron Bradshaw replaced Barney Oldfield as referee. Wagner remained as starter as did technical judge George Stephenson. R. R. Johnson was named clerk of course. Harold Hooks was chief scorer. Roy E. Tuttle, chief timer and Bill Claus, pit manager. Departmentally, H. H. Beall replaced Pickens as publicist when Pickens departed for other fortunes. Sgt. Ed McAlliffe was director of police. W. H. Ward was scoreboard director. Rising & Son took over the concessions. The Legion's George Hammond was supervisor of tickets. Head usher was R. E. Eaton. The Legion band still provided the music.

Harper Radio Service furnished public address equipment and "Pop" Evans led the maintenance crew. Herb Marow handled the radio commentary.

The Legion's Executive Board was Dr. Loring, chairman; George Hammond, Harry Schmidt and W. H. "Reg" Regelin, in charge of programming. All races remained under AAA sanction.

Among the drivers at that time were Gelston, Sharp, Bundy, Mel McKee, Heisler, Carl Ryder, Hinkley, Stubblefield, Brunmier, Cliff Wilson, Bud Hyatt, Chris Vest, Woody Woodford, Walt May, Art Boyce, Harry Jacquez, Fred Merzney, Pete Nosik, Nick Martino, Al Gordon, Pete Nielson, Guy Deulin, Dewey Skipworth, Quinn, Ed Moody and others.

Some of the speed plants were "Frontys," Chevys, Rajos, Cragars and others. Among the "Specials" being driven were Mahoney, Mikkelson, Redlands, Miller and the Hooker.

On Wednesday night, June 15, Jimmy Sharp won the 50-lap main event before 10,000 fans, with McKee second, Quinn, third. Charley Gelston won the "Helmet Dash" and a big kiss from starlet Peggy Hamilton. Nick Martino spun on the north turn and blasted the fence repeatedly before halting on the track in the main event. Ryder, Bundy and Brunmier won heat races.

The 15-cent program was loaded with pictures and ads, one which read: "Simplex wins again" (Simplex Piston Rings). Another read: Winfield (carburetors) wins at Indianapolis. Western Gasoline (as stated by the Caraba Wynn Oil Co.), read: "Use Tru-Lube Motor Oil."

Otto K. Olesen Illuminating Co., of Hollywood, which installed lighting equipment at the track, also placed an ad under the title, "We Light the World." The ad read: "The light was perfect as I was able to see 100 per cent at all times." The ad was signed by Nick Martino, winner of the main event of the first night racing program on June 29, 1927.

The program also included a feature story on chief scorer H. L. (Harold) Hook, telling of his duties as chief scorer at old Beverly Hills board speedway. A civil engineer, Hook had assisted Pillsbury in building the Culver City board track and many others.

By June 29, 1929, there was a slight change in Ascot management. Early day racing pioneer Frank Verbeck replaced Theron Bradshaw as referee and Norman J. Hartford took over the publicity chores from II. H. Beall. Hartford was an ambitious young man who was a protege of the departed Bill Pickens. Hartford was imaginative as Pickens, and his talent gave the Legion a tremendous boost in publicity.

Driver lineups remained about the same with the exceptions that McKee replaced Stubblefield in the No. 18 "Simplex Piston Ring Special." Sonny Gleason, a good driver, grabbed the "Howard Special" No. 30 "Fronty." Floyd Stump snatched the No. 49 "Fronty Ford Special." Mel Miller was assigned the No. 51 "Fronty Special" and Al Meniam drove his own "Meniam Special" No. 88.

June 29 the management scheduled a 50-lap main event which was won by Bill Heisler in a "Fronty" Ford. Sharp finished second, followed by Carl Ryder. Francis Quinn won the Helmet Dash and a kiss from actress Genevieve Tobin. Heat winners were Brunmier, Hyatt, Vest and Martino. The attendance was 9,500.

While Kenealy was leading the chase to the 1929 title, Quinn got his "Dayton Thorobred Special" 91 cubic inch Miller into high gear and pressed Kenealy. Quinn, after a slow start, during which he lagged far behind the leaders, rallied for his stirring second place finish. Charley Gelston was third and Ernie Triplett, fourth.

In winning the title Kenealy received the Simplex Piston Ring Trophy along with a cash award. Kenealy, a colorful character, was known as "that Chinaman." Oldtimers recall Mel having worked in a Chinese laundry and, on occasions, signed autographs in Chinese!

Ascot was the scene of excitement and thrills during those days and one fan was heard to express his enthusiasm by saying:

"Some people like baseball . . . others like football . . . I'll take mine here." His exuberance clearly described the action at Ascot during those nerve-shattering days of 1928 and 1929. Speed and action were at high pitch.

An example of the intensity among the drivers was displayed July 4, 1929, during a special 100 lap Declaration Day Sweepstakes before 12,000 screaming fans.

The main participants in the feature event were Triplett and Quinn who put on such a dazzling display of daring and courageous driving, they kept the excited crowd standing for the entire race. Ernie would grab the lead then Quinn would charge in front as the pair sailed hub-to-hub into the turns and back on the straightaways with neither giving ground. Ernie and Francis traded the lead no less than nine times as they battled inches from the guardrail at more than 100 miles per hour.

On two occasions, with only the width of a radiator shell separating the two cars, officials at the starting line scurried for cover because they thought the speedsters would crash against the officials' stand. Others feared that the speed-crazed drivers might lock wheels and hurtle the racers into the grandstand, maim themselves and some spectators. The hub-to-hub duel went on for several more laps before Quinn, the "Bald Eagle," finally nosed out Triplett after a race considered by many as the most thrilling they had ever witnessed. The fans gasped for air and talked about the display of speed and daringness for many days after. Sure enough, Triplett, Quinn and the other intrepid drivers would be back for more speed in future American Legion promoted programs.

American Legion Speedway would remain as the official name of the track until the 1933 racing season, when the change-over to LEGION ASCOT SPEEDWAY would occur. However, loyal fans always called the oval "Ascot" because of the original title established by builder George R. Bentel in 1924.

American Legion Race Board of Control

Legion
Ascot
Speedway

American Legion Race Board of Control. No. 1 through 10 are: Dr. Fred Loring, W. King Provan, Gene Gilliland, Henry Prussing, John Lichtig, "Reg" Regelin, Edgar Johnson, Harry Schmidt, Bob Rawley, Walter Richards. (Courtesy Roscoe Turner.)

American Legion Band, Post 127, of Glendale, California, was a spirited group which kept the fans in a happy mood between races. Here conductor George Kryder leads a bit of marching on the straightaway before the start of another sizzling program. (Courtesy Roscoe Turner.)

Snappy looking American Automobile Association officials gave Ascot touch of class. Art Pillsbury, Western Region director, is fifth from left. Picture taken on main straightaway. (Courtesy Roscoe Turner.)

The backbone of Ascot's success is represented in a gathering of some officials on the main straightaway, on the starting line. From left, front, are George Hammond and Dr. Fred Loring, American Legion Post 127, of Glendale, California; Art Pillsbury, Western Region director of the AAA; Kenny Paine of the Legion, and Fred "Pop" Wagner, perhaps the most famous race starter in the sport's history. At extreme left is Reg Regelin, also of Post 127. The year: 1928.

Ascot, in those days, had its share of hotdog vendors. You could buy a foot-long "dog" for a dime. They were known as "red hots" to the hungry fans. Ascot's grandstand stood high, as noted in background. Any of these vendors around today??? (Courtesy Roscoe Turner.)

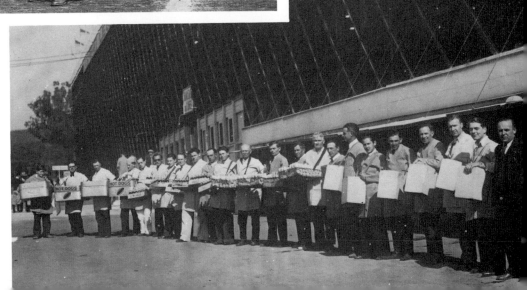

"Bald Eagle" Francis Quinn in the "Schmidt Special," 1929. Mechanic Earl Evans (center). Les Quinn, right. Man at left is unidentified.

Pete DePaulo, 1925 Indianapolis winner, visited the Ascot pits and posed for this picture with Francis Quinn. The "Bald Eagle" was enroute to the 1930 Pacific Southwest championship. The car is Russ Garnant's SR rocker arm Fronty "Gabhart Special." The street car is a Reo "Flying Cloud."

(Doug Boyd collection.)

Francis Quinn, left, and Walt May were great friends off the track. On the track, however, was a different situation. Quinn shows off his new $6,000 "Francis Quinn Special," while May sits in the "Dayton Thorobred Special" in which Quinn won the 1930 Pacific Southwest championship. It's February, 1931, just five months before May's fatal wreck at San Jose. Quinn died on the highway in December.

Otto Lind in his "Lind Special." Warming for a night race on February 20, 1927.

Herman Schurch was a tough driver . . . matching strength and energy with Ascot's best. Herman was top ranking driver for 1930, but died on the speedpaths in 1931. Picture taken September 27, 1927.

Who drove the "Land Special" No. 3? Could the "driver" be a motion picture actor filming a flicker, say about 1927?

Majority of pictures appearing in this book can be obtained from the collection of Bruce Craig, 401 New Jersey Ave., Phillipsburg, N.

Walt May, before his death at San Jose in 1931, was a terrific driver at Ascot. May, no doubt, paid little heed to the unprotected battery lying beside his "Multi-Ford Special." That's "Stubby" Stubblefield (hands behind back) in rear. Car No. 45 is Bob Scovel's "India Special." Car No. 20 is the "Dink Special" driven by Arvol Brunmier during this 1929 Ascot day.

Walt May, left, "Dayton Thorobred Special," and Francis Quinn, "Francis Quinn Special," during 1931 Saturday practice day at Ascot.

Jimmy Sharp encountered trouble with his Fronty during a 1929 Ascot race. Jimmy was one of few drivers to wear a kidney belt. The car is the "Mahoney Special," single cam S-R Fronty, with Model T Ford block.

(Left)
The two front cars are perfectly abreast as veteran starter Fred "Pop" Wagner waves the field away on January 2, 1930. Walt May is on the pole. Other throttle pushers are unidentified. May went on to win the 75-lap main on the opening day of the season.

(Right)
"Stubby" Stubblefield has his way during this June 9, 1930 "Helmet Dash," besting Francis Quinn at a rapid clip. Stubblefield tools Russ Garnant's "Gabhart Special," while Quinn guns the "Dayton Thorobred Special." Francis turned the tables on gold-tooth "Stubby" in the 100-lap feature, however, and held the lead the entire distance!

(Left)
"Get outta the way . . . give me room," Shorty Cantlon could have been thinking, as he grabbed the lead coming out of Ascot's north turn on February 5, 1930. Pillars outside the fence were supports for the old (and temporary) grandstand which was used only one racing season. That's Lou Moore in second place. "Stubby" Stubblefield is breathing Lou's exhaust fumes.

(Right)
Find the third one . . . he's in there but tied up like the weekly wash. Walt May is on this side, Ernie Triplett in the middle, Francis Quinn on the inside. When this trio floorboarded the throttle, something had to "give."

A wreck . .. fire . . . and death. Youthful and aspiring Long Beach drive Kenny Morgan met his end in this smashup on December 14, 1930. Shorty Cantlon won the main event that ill-fated day.

Kenny Morgan is about to be placed on a stretcher after his fiery wreck on Ascot's main straightaway on December 14, 1930.

A somersaulting Model-T winds up over the south turn fence. This time it was Dud Ludwick's turn to face the Grim Reaper. April 17, 1927.

Harry Jacquez suffered a broken back after his car plowed through the north turn fence in 1928. The "Redlands Special" sustained severe damage.   (Doug Boyd collection.)

Ascot almost claimed another courageous driver in the wreck of the "American Special" in 1930. Driver Lester Spangler barely escaped death, although he was severely injured, after the car shot over the south turn fence and slammed down the 25-foot embankment. Note the crumbled front end of the car.

This car blasted the wire fencing near the Ascot infield. Driver of the "Weber Special" is unidentified. Was car owner George Weber behind the wheel?

Chet Gardner bent up his No. 12 in this Ascot wreak after the car threw a piece of wood into the grandstand and struck a youth. The boy's injuries were fatal. Gardner was slightly hurt. Note inner tubes poking out of front wheels.

"This car had a 4-cylinder, 191 cubic inch Miller Marine engine . . . it was one of the first Millers in regular competition at Ascot," Arvol Brunmier, seated in the "Piston Ring Shop Special," said. Brunmier, known as the "Whittier Shiek," is pictured in 1930.

"Stubby" Stubblefield seated in the "Redlands Special" with car owner Eddie Meyer standing alongside. Site is Ascot Speedway, 1929. (Courtesy Roscoe Turner.)

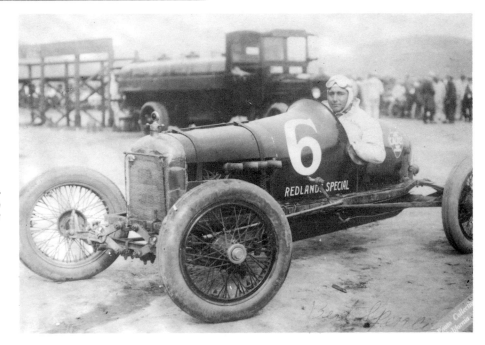

New Mexican Bert Spencer and his "Redlands Special.' Spencer won the first all single seat 100 lapper at Ascot in 1927. This Fronty Ford was a hairy car for its time.

George Souders in the "Duesenberg Special" in which he won the 1927 Indianapolis race. Souders brought this car to Ascot on December 8, 1927, seven months after his big victory. Souders drove Ascot prior to 1927, and was a big attraction.

Ascot racing cars came big and brawny, as Ted Simpson's powerful 12-cylinder Chrysler indicates. March 13, 1927, is the day. Side springs probably were less effective in handling, for the boys would soon switch to cross-springs.

"Speed" Hinkley seated in Lloyd Vieux's big Miller. It's the "Vieux Special," a regular entry at Ascot.

Mel McKee, who lived in Maywood, California, posed alongside the "PAR Special" in 1931. The SR Rocker Arm Fronty was formerly known as the "Gabhart Special," which Francis Quinn drove to the 1930 Pacific Southwest title. Russ Garnant was the chief mechanic and Lou Moore of "Blue Crown" fame built the speedster.

(Doug Boyd collection.)

Far as Arvol Brunmier was concerned, the "Whittier Shiek" would drive anything on wheels. The "Up-Cyl Oil Special" Model-A was of no exception. It's a 1928 race day at Ascot. The car, however, had the more "modern" cross springs which were introduced at Ascot by famed Eddie Meyer.

(Courtesy Roscoe Turner.)

A young and ambitious Ernie Triplett is pictured in 1929 in Barney Kloepfer's "Barney Special" at Ascot. Triplett was later dubbed the "Blond Terror" and the "Belvedere Badboy" for his electrifying driving. Triplett was 1931-32 champion.

Ernie Triplett as he looked in 1929. He was known at that time as the "Belvedere Badboy" for his heroics on the speed-paths.

Art Pillsbury, AAA Western Region director who also designed many board speedways during the 1920s. Pillsbury, highly respected by the racing fraternity, was very influential in Ascot's steady climb to national prominence.

(Courtesy Roscoe Turner.)

Cliff Bergere at Ascot on April 2, 1929. He pressed Mel Kenealy for Southwest honors that year.

Gus Schrader, an Ascot veteran who for years was known as the "king of the dirt tracks" until he met his untimely death at Shreveport, Louisiana.

Bill Red" Heisler, Ascot favorite from 1924 to 1930. Heisler was killed on the Fresno, California, mile dirt track in 1931. This is Bill on July 12, 1929.

George Souders was a great dirt track driver and an outstanding driver at Ascot. Souders won the 1927 Indianapolis 500.

Francis Quinn was driving the bee-jabbers out of the "Dayton Thorobred Special" at Ascot in 1929. A championship wasn't too far distant for the "Bald Eagle."

Former vegetable truck driver Kelly Petillo who started racing at Ascot in 1927. Kelly was a splendid driver who won the 1935 Indianapolis 500.

"Shorty" Cantlon when he first appeared at Ascot in 1929. The Detroit, Michigan driver was killed at Indianapolis In 1947.

Bill White, owner of Ernie Triplett's famous "Red Lion Special" championship car. White promoted the last two races at Ascot Speedway, featuring two-man Indianapolis cars, 1935.-36

(Courtesy Roscoe Turner.)

Lester Spangler, standout Ascot driver. He died at Indianapolis in 1933.

Ascot favorite, Bill Spence. Bill crashed to his death at Indianapolis in 1929.

The 1929 Pacific Southwest champion . . . Mel Kenealy. It's the "Padres Special," a 191 cubic inch Miller. It's also the 1930 racing season at Ascot, and Mel proudly carries the No. 1. The car was sponsored by the Vai Brothers of Cucamonga, California. The fur draped lady? Who knows.

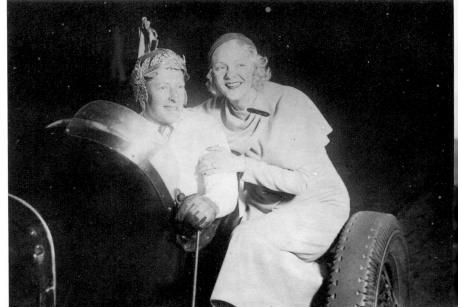

Intrepid Carl Ryder receives victory crown after "Helmet Dash" win, 1930.

Kelly Petillo, who won the 1935 Indianapolis 500, shows off his baby shoes—a lucky charm, he says— while seated in the "Triflex Special" Fronty Ford speedster at Ascot. It was main event time on December 16, 1928.

A novel electric timing device, invented locally, is in use at the Legion Ascot Speedway and has proved so successful that it will be used, so 'tis said, at Indianapolis and other speedways. A beam of light shines across the track. Here starter Fred Wagner (right) and Dr. Fred Loring are shown inspecting the projector. (Ascot Speedway, 1931).

H.R. Harper, inventor of the novel device, is shown at his post in the judges' stand, surrounded by stop watches, telephones and suchlike paraphernalia. The timing system had proved to be remarkably accurate in registering the speed of race cars. January 24, 1931.

The light beam across the track in focused upon a sensitive electric cell. When the speeding cars cut across the light beam—as here shown—the break in the circuit, so to speak, caused that sensitive cell to open and close, as light is cut off. The opening and closing of the sensitive cell operates a circuit that starts and stops electric watches in the timer's box. "Stubby" Stubblefield in No. 7 and Ralph DePalma, No. 1, roar across finish line in this test. January 24, 1931.

Another guessing game. More identities are needed here. We know the year was 1927, but who are the mechanics and driver? Can anybody help?

Bill Hart and his "Rotary Valve Special" during a Wednesday night racing card at Ascot in 1930. Car owner Bill Weir stands alongside.

"This straightaway is mine" could be Ernie Triplett's thoughts as he leads Carl Ryder at 90 miles per hours at Ascot on December 21, 1929. Ernie is tooling Barney Kloepfer's "Kloepfer Special." Who's that smoking in the rear, by the way?

(Left)
Francis Quinn, No. 8 "Dayton Thorobred Special," tries to get between unidentified driver (left) and Nick Martino in car No. 7, as the cars head into the dangerous south turn. Quinn was speeding towards the 1930 Pacific Southwest championship.

(Right)
A grinning Kenny Stoddard at starting line for heat race in the "Calpet Gasoline Special" in 1927. Strapped down hood, a "hanging" battery, side mounted (and exposed) oil tank . . . it doesn't matter. Of course, crash helmets were unheard of then. But the word "action" was familiar to all.

Exposed and unprotected rear gasoline tank made little difference to Bill Bundy. "Let's race" was the only reply of the cigar chewing, nervy dirt track star. Bundy's "Dizzy 100 Special" made plenty of drivers dizzy with his death defying driving. A crash helmet? "I never heard of one," he'd say today. It's race day at Ascot, September 27, 1927.

(Right)
"Move over boy, I'm comin' atcha," Francis Quinn could possibly have said, as he zeroed in on Walt May in the No. 3 "Dayton Thorobred Special" going into the south turn. Quinn tools the "Gabhart Special" in which he won the 1930 Pacific Southwest championship.   (Courtesy Roscoe Turner.)

Francis Quinn on January 12, 1929. Not yet a champion, but plenty ambitious. He drove in Ascot's first race in 1924, was champ in 1930.

Actress Sally Blaine (she's Loretta Young's sister) places the Victory Crown helmet upon Kelly Petillo after a 1929 "Helmet Dash" win. Petillo, in Ascot action since 1927, is in the "Tri-flex Special" Fronty Ford. Kelly won the 1935 Indianapolis Speedway race.

Francis Quinn shows off the Dick Dodd Memorial Trophy for winning the 1930 Pacific Southwest title. He also holds the Best Appearing Car and Crew trophy presented by the AAA. The car is Russ Garnant's No. 2 "Gabhart Special."

(Courtesy Al and Gertrude Dorcey.)

Mel McKee, right, shows Ernie Triplett how to plant a heavy foot on the accelerator pedal of a racing car. No doubt Triplett needed little instruction. August 27, 1931.

Harold (Jack) Petticord, who drove at Ascot Speedway during the 1920s. (Courtesy Roscoe Turner.)

Lynn Eldridge was another promising driver whose career was cut short in a fatal Ascot wreck on October 15, 1930. (Courtesy Roscoe Turner.)

Lou Moore, left, and Mel Kenealy smile confidently . . . hoping to overcome the front-drive Millers of Leon Duray, No. 12, and Cliff Bergere, No. 24. It was an exhibition event for the big Indy cars of the day, February 11, 1928.

Cliff Bergere in action during a warm-up on January 14, 1928. The car is a front-drive 8-cylinder Miller powered mount. Cliff for years held the Indianapolis record for number of laps completed there during racing competition. Bergere was an Ascot standout from 1927 to 1929.

On a dirt track, Gus Schrader was tough to beat. Ask any veteran racing driver. Schrader is pictured at Ascot in 1930 . . . a top ranking driver that year. Gus met his end in a terrific smashup at Shreveport, Louisiana, 1938. (Alvarez-Craig.)

William "Shorty" Cantlon in a familiar Ascot pose on November 10, 1930. Cantlon lost his life at Indianapolis in 1947.

Babe Stapp at the wheel of the "Bobby Special," a Fronty Ford he drove at Ascot during the 1928 season.

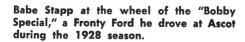

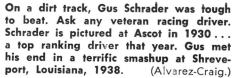

Unidentified drivers thunder down Ascot's main straight-away, about 1928.

Zoom . . . "Stubby" Stubblefield receives checkered flag from a waving veteran starter, Fred "Pop" Wagner, on March 25, 1930.

Steppin' on the gas and letting 'er rip for a "hard start." Supposedly a four abreast start, race finally got underway, with Francis Quinn (left, outside) winning. Ed Winfield is No. 1, is his two up and two down "T" flathead. Bill Spence is in Harry Hooker's DO Miller "T" No. 99.   (Doug Boyd collection.)

Action on the homestretch going into Ascot's dangerous south turn, Wilbur Shaw, No. 48 "Blue-Green Special" leads, with Babe Stapp, Francis Quinn and Ernie Triplett following behind. Quinn won the 100-lap main event.

(Courtesy Roscoe Turner.)

Ascot underwent some minor changes in 1928, with the installation of markers on the inside of the north turn. Wide inner apron indicates that the turn was narrowed, only to be reinstated later to its original width. Bill Spence in No. 8 leads unidentified driver.

(Courtesy Roscoe Turner.)

George Souders, 1927 Indianapolis winner, made an impromtu but successful appearance at Ascot, a year after he won the Memorial Day event. Here he leads Frame around the dirt north turn on April 10, 1928. Frame was to win at Indianapolis four years later.

Everybody is unidentified in this old Ascot photo. Who are they? Please, somebody, pick out these boys.

Nick Martino, whose promising career was cut short when he was killed during a driving exhibition in a vacant field in Hollywood, 1932. Martino is pictured at Ascot in 1930.

Bob Scovel hailed from Portland, Oregon, and tried his wares at Ascot in 1929. Scovel was a terror in the Land of the Green and stood just as tall in Ascot competition. Bob's in the "Rajo Special" in 1930.

CHAPTER III

QUINN, TRIPLETT DUEL

(1928 - 1931)

"Bald Eagle," A Champion

Wheel-to-Wheel Rivalry

Ascot's "Big Six"

Brushing the Fence

Jimmy Sharp's Misfortune

East-West Match Races

Ryder Black Flagged

"Red Pete" Goes Sour

"The Crowd Roars"

Colorful "Wild Bill"

The captivating and colorful history of Ascot Speedway, as noted earlier, can be defined in five simple terms:

A—acceleration. S—suspense. C—courage. O—obsession. T—thrills.

Francis Quinn and Ernie Triplett were perhaps the most representative of those descriptive terms, by which the famous auto racing track was so aptly identified.

Quinn and Triplett were the best of friends off the track. But once they were rolling on Ascot's speedpaths, all friendship was forgotten and it was strictly a "you're gonna have to beat me" challenge.

When Quinn and Triplett hooked up in one of their scorching duels, the fans would pack the grandstand and crowd the infield parking area, because they KNEW they were about to witness some sensational driving by two truly great drivers on a notoriously dangerous track.

Beginning January 1, 1930, and with the American Legion in full command of the newly-named American Legion Speedway, the management announced the inclusion of a new set of flag signals to be used for the current season and in the future.

Whereas in previous years when only the starting green, the yellow caution and the checkered finish flags were used during contests, included for the new year was the red flag (stop race immediately) white flag (stop at pit, consult with referee) orange with blue center flag (you're not giving overtaking car right-of-way) and king blue flag (one more lap to go).

Perhaps it was ironic, or even coincidental, that the orange with blue center flag would be utilized beginning with the 1930 racing season, because the flag became a "must" considering the way Quinn and Triplett threw caution to the wind in their heated rivalry.

Oldtimers remember how often the orange with blue center flag was waved during their duels, telling one driver or the other that he wasn't giving the overtaking car the right-of-way. It simply meant that Triplett and Quinn were stubbornly refusing to yield the right-of-way to the other guy (according to the rules). Theirs was a race for the 1930 championship, and many times were in no mood to pay heed to the move-over flag. The pair risked being suspended, and they somehow got away with it.

Francis and Ernie would practically force some drivers off the track when they put their rivalry into high gear, unless the other guys were members of Ascot's "big six". The "big six," in those awesome 1930 racing days, besides Triplett and Quinn, were Walt May, Jimmy Sharp, Arvol Brunmier and "Stubby" Stubblefield. These six speed demons, aggressive as they were, also found rugged opposition in the likes of Chet Gardner, Speed Hinkley, Mel McKee, former motorcycle racer Johnny Kreiger, Herman Schurch, 1929 champion Mel Kenealy, Shorty Cantlon and Carl Ryder.

Cantlon, a little 5-foot 2 fellow from Detroit, began his racing career in 1922 in Michigan County fairs. He had signed to drive Bill White's rear-disc wheel "Miller Special" in 1929. Despite being 1929 champion, Kenealy couldn't get enough power out of his "Padre Special" No. 1 championship car to cope with the "Big Six." Yet, slender Mel displayed plenty of moxie while making it "hot" for the front-runners before departing in mid-season for eastern and midwestern tracks.

For the January 18 program, however, Sharp, May and Stubblefield were billed as the "Three Musketeers of the Speedway" for their 1-2-3 finishes in the two previous main events. The pre-race publicity paid off handsomely as more than 10,000 fans watched Sharp in Russ Garnant's "Gabhart Special" out-duel his two adversaries for his third consecutive main event victory.

Yet, it was Quinn and Triplett who would dominate the action, whether in a "Helmet Dash," heat race or main event. The pair, pitted in the "Dash," was something to see, because they'd have the whole track to themselves. Actually, Quinn was an unassuming individual whose character typified the highest of living standards. His sportsmanship and friendly attitude, courage, competitive spirit and ability made him the toast of Ascot in 1930. He was crowned Pacific Southwest champion for achieving the most points, received a generous cash award and several trophies, thus earning admiration equal to the legendary Ralph DePalma and the great Frank Lockhart.

Quinn had driven at Ascot since the opening season and soon became a big favorite with the fans. He was a master car builder, as well, and didn't smoke or drink. In the minds of drivers and fans, Quinn was a real champion.

The intrepid Triplett had one passion: SPEED.

Ernie also was a gentleman who considered everyone his friend. In fact he was known to use the polite noun, "Sir!" whether he spoke to minor or elder.

Triplett had the strongest desire to succeed on a race track. Besides wanting to win the Pacific Southwest title, his main ambition was to win the Indianapolis Speedway race. The passion to win the "500" dogged him to his end. He never won at Indy; his best finsh was seventh in 1931. The ex-motorcycle racer who got his start at Banning Speedway, had driven at Ascot since 1926. Perhaps it was coincidental that when Ernie was "getting hot" at Ascot in 1928, Quinn was there to meet his challenge. That's where the rivalry began.

Triplett, like his arch rival Quinn, was highly admired and had many followers, like "Arnie's Army" which flocked after the legendary Arnold Palmer on the golfing circuit. Triplett was a class driver who showed many competitors how to handle a racing car.

The bitterness of the Quinn-Triplett feud clearly indicated that Ascot was no place for amateurs or conservative drivers who chose to pace themselves and hopefully come on and win. Ascot was a track for the aggressor. Either a driver stuck his neck out in the dangerous atmosphere, or he had to settle for last place. That's how fierce the competition was.

Oldtime mechanic "Red" Garnant added the following tale to the Quinn-Triplett rivalry:

"At times Triplett seemed to get the advantage over Quinn with a special second gear installed in the transmission of the Billy Arnold-owned "Miller Special" No. 40. It was in the "Helmet Dash" one day when Quinn, Triplett and Arvol Brunmier were jocking for position. About 100 feet from the starting line Triplett, on the pole, would control the race. Brunmier and Quinn would keep pace in high gear to assure an even start. However, once at the starting line Triplett would shift into high and accelerate into the lead, never to be headed. Meanwhile, Quinn and Brunmier, their "Fronty" Fords already in high gear, would fall behind and have no chance.

'We'll fix him,' "Quinn later told Arvol. Sure enough, the following racing program saw Triplett in the "Helmet Dash" with Brunmier and Quinn. This time, though, instead of Ernie on the pole position and controlling the start, it was Quinn who had the accelerating advantage. Quinn refused to slow the pace. Instead, he accelerated into high gear at the starting line. Triplett, keeping pace, blew his engine when shifting into high gear. Quinn and Brunmier finished 1-2. Knowing the trick wouldn't work unless he was on the pole (which wasn't always), Triplett installed a conventional speed box thereafter for future races."

Midway in 1930, when Quinn and Triplett took turns beating each other, this question echoed among fans:

Were Quinn and Triplett really bitter rivals on the track, or was it just a put-up show as a publicity stunt? Certainly they drove like they wanted to force the other over the fence, so aggressive was their driving which left the fans exhausted from the excitement.

Norman Hartford who had replaced H. H. Beall as publicity writer, described how he had arranged the fabled "Quinn-Triplett rivalry."

"For publicity, I once drummed up a feud between Triplett and Quinn that could have had homicidal results. One or the other would win each week with the driver taking second place following the lead car so close the front wheels actually rubbed paint off the front car. It was a competitive one-two week so I, as publicity man, rigged up a verbal battle between the two.

'If Triplett doesn't move over and let me pass I'll push him over,' said Quinn (I quoted him in the newspapers).

'If he starts that I'll show him the rough stuff I learned on eastern dirt tracks,' answered Triplett, 'I'll do some pushing myself.' (I also quoted Ernie in the papers).

"Came the night of the next race and Harry Hartz, oldtime driver, walked up to me in the office of the track and said: 'Do you realize these guys believe what they saw in the papers. They're ready to kill each other out there. Mechanics and hangers-on in their garages have been ribbing them about the stories and they are both hot under the collar.'

"I decided to cross the track and cool them off, explaining it was press agent stuff to arouse interest and attract a crowd. But it was too late, the main event had started and there were Triplett and Quinn in the front row sneering at each other with mean, determined looks on their faces. Starter Fred Wagner waved them away and my heart missed a few beats. If one of them got killed I was sure as hell responsible.

"They caught the starting flag at 110 mph and thundered into the fatal south turn, neck and neck.

"Then the unexpected and anti-climax happened. Triplett's motor threw a rod, the car slowed and he drifted from the pack to the lower inside of the track. The danger was over.

"You can be sure I talked the pair out of any bad blood and hot-tempered feelings before the next race," Hartford concluded.

Actually, neither driver had said a word which would have embroiled hatred toward the other. After the publicity stunt had been explained and tempers cooled, Quinn and Triplett continued their hectic desire to beat the other, regardless.

Here's an example:

One night Triplett grabbed the lead in heavy traffic. Quinn, in second place, began to close on Ernie and finally was hounding his screeching rear tires in laps that averaged 26 seconds. Quinn made several desperate attempts to pass, but Ernie gamely held the lead. "If he doesn't move over this time I'll tear his wheels off," Quinn seemed to say. This went on for several laps. Then they came together, wheel to wheel. Triplett's car brushed against Quinn's and they almost locked wheels at more than 100 mph, inches from the outside fence. Quinn, somehow, came out best and jumped into the lead. The crowd roared.

Francis held on for 10 gruelling laps and

won, with Ernie right at his exhaust pipe. The fans were sure they would settle their differences with fisticuffs, but they came out of the pits arm-in-arm and smiling like old pals—which they really were. Quinn set a 40-lap record of 18.16 seconds that night.

Carl Ryder got into the Quinn-Triplett fuss in a 100 lapper the following Sunday afternoon. There were 10,000 fans to see the usual: Triplett and Quinn trading the lead, with Wilbur Shaw, Stubby, Sharp, May and the rest trying to keep close. Francis and Ernie were about to pass Ryder when Carl's car snapped an oil line and spread gooey stuff all over the back stretch. Ryder was black flagged but he refused to come in. Officials at the starting line became furious. Again they waved the black flag, again Ryder refused.

Triplett and Shaw, speeding down the back straightaway, spun in the oil. Triplett brushed the fence and Shaw hit the infield after a wild spin. The fearless Quinn didn't touch a thing and weaving through the spinning cars, zoomed on to win again. The crowd gasped relief in that no serious accident had been touched off. Ryder, meanwhile, drew a 30-day suspension. In less than 30 days, though, Carl somehow returned to action.

Soon after there was another night:

Triplett, Quinn and Arvol Brunmier were pouring it on, with Ernie in front before a capacity crowd of 12,000. Arvol experienced some bad luck in his Miller Marine speedster, and was soon out of the running. This put Ernie and Francis 1-2 at break-neck speeds down the straights and on the turns, with their rear wheels brushing just inches from the outside fence. There was danger in the air. Finally Triplett lost the lead on the dangerous south turn when Quinn threw caution to the wind and passed him, but Ernie dipped low in the turn and regained the lead all in one swoosh! Triplett held on to win, with the "Bald Eagle's" front wheels at Ernie's exhaust pipe. Triplett erased Quinn's 40-lap record by a 100th of a second! The fans went wild.

Two weeks later the American Legion scheduled a special five-lap match race between the East and West stars. Shaw and Bill Cummings represented the East and the National circuit. Quinn and Walt May, the West and Pacific Southwest AAA. Shaw and "Wild Bill" set a hot pace and won the event, finishing one-two. The western stars begged for a rematch. They got it five weeks later. This time Quinn and Triplett teamed up and turned the tables on the easterners Shaw and Cummings. Quinn and Ernie finished one-two, with the "Bald Eagle's" Miller powered "Dayton Thorobred Special" accelerating hot and smooth. Triplett's "Allen Special" No. 6 also purred to perfection that afternoon.

At this time the management was doing its best to publicize its racing stars in the papers. One headline read, "Present Auto Racers Likened to Former Stars." Below the heading, pictures compared Triplett to Leon Duray as spectacular, Quinn to Tommy Milton as crafty, Stubblefield to Harry Hartz as steady, and Arvol Brunmier to Ralph DePalma as colorful.

The management also helped create new fans by admitting them free on Saturdays and Tuesday, the days before regular race days. Fans could watch the drivers practice turning some hot laps. The unveiling of a new car was always exciting.

Free admission to watch the drivers practice had terrific impact, and admiration for the drivers soared. In a warmup session the fans could see some beautiful cars and enough action to entice them to attend the races. They also got a chance to enter the pits and chat with the drivers and seek autographs.

The 1930 season was a spectacular one. Quinn switched from his "Dayton Thorobred Special" to Russ Garnant's "Gabhart Special" to win the Pacific Southwest title. Quinn obtained the Garnant car when Jimmy Sharp, its regular driver who led briefly in point standings, fractured his arm in a smashup at Bakersfield. Jimmy returned too soon—before his arm was at full strength—and was killed in his next race on the newly-opened Oakland mile. Quinn was then assigned the "Gabhart" permanently.

In those days most of the cars used Dayton tires. The tread would be planed off with a tire turning machine to provide better traction on the dirt oil surface. A blend of 20 per cent Benzol and 80 per cent high octane gasoline gave the cars plenty of pep.

Many of the "rail jobs" carried two hooks hanging from the front axle beneath the car on each side of the body as a safety precaution. If a spindle broke or a car threw a wheel the hooks would dig into the track's surface and prevent the axle from digging into the track and cause the car to flip. Ace mechanic Paul Weirick stated, however, "This safety device was okay on the straightaways . . . very ineffective taking the turns at high speed . . . wasn't long before the boys started removing the hooks."

By 1930, all drivers frowned on carrying the numeral 13 on their cars. However, Tony Radetich drove the "Dugan Special" No. 13 in 1929. Otto Lind also drove his own "Lind Special" No. 13 in 1928. Although Radetich and Lind escaped serious accidents, the drivers soon adhered to the old racing superstition and no numeral 13 would be seen again at Ascot. It is recalled that a car carrying No. 13 at another track, had crashed with fatal results. Thus the superstition took effect at Ascot.

Ascot's January 26, 1930, program offered a bit of excitement involving Fred Merzney, driving a No. 12 "Fronty Special." Merzney spun on the south turn, crashed into the fence and turned over. When the dust had cleared Merzney could be seen lying underneath the car, but he rested on his forehead with only a broken thumb. Merzney always drove with a good luck charm (a cigar stuck in his chops), but for some reason, drove without the stogie in the race he was injured.

A short story in the program indicated an effort to raise $12,000 in lap money for various meets during 1930. It was agreed that $5 per lap, by donor, would be given to the driver leading the main event. "Donors should call Mr. Roy Tuttle at Oregon 1515," the story read. The plan succeeded and carried through future seasons.

Another notation in the program of January 26, 1930: "By track management order, no solicitations; no begging; no sales of pencils, cards, flowers, etc., in the grandstand or on speedway grounds. Please report all violators to Ascot office."

Also in the program was a feature story on pit manager Bill Claus, telling of his racing exploits against Earl Cooper, Joe Dawson, Roscoe Sarles, Dario Resta, Eddie Hearne and Barney Oldfield—all great drivers of an earlier era.

Another change among the officials was effective February 9, 1930. Two-time Indianapolis winner and former national champion Tommy Milton replaced Frank Verbeck as referee for one month. Bill Koller took over as chief starter from the retired Fred "Pop" Wagner. Other changes saw Pat Holland and Walter Hansen instilled as technical inspectors, Dick Doyle assisting chief timer Roy Tuttle, veteran driver Cliff Bergere replacing Bill Claus as pit manager. Three assistant scorers, Fred Betz, G. S. G. Patterson and E. G. Beth, joined head scorer H. L. Cook.

Dr. Loring remained chairman of the

entire Legion force, assisted by an executive board comprised of E. R. Johnson, E. Fred Franklin. Harry Schmidt and W. H. Richards.

The February 9, 1930, night racing program included motorcycle racing. Entries were Miny Waln, Ralph Stalnaker, Tuffie Jacobs, Bob Newman, Cliff Hill, P. A. Bigsby, "Dusty" Rhodes, all driving Indians; Bill Richter, Henry Rhodes, R. Stafford, Tex Bryant, H. Pelton, Ben Gille and Bob Briggs, all on Harley-Davidson mounts. Art Olson entered with an Excelsior. There were also side car and sole events.

Racing car drivers entered included Ernie Triplett, "Barney Special" No. 33; Quinn, "Dayton Thorobred Special" No. 8; "Shorty Cantlon, "Schofield Miller Special" No. 18; Fred Frame, Miller; Tony Radetich, "Dugan Special" No. 39 (Tony had sidetracked No. 13) ; George Conners, M. O. Babb, Kelly Petillo and Johnny Kreiger, among others.

Leading drivers were Cantlon, 63.37 points; Stubblefield, 54.85; Swede Smith, Krieger, Mel McKee, Phil Pardee, Charley Gelston, Frame, Herman Schurch and down to Carl Ryder, 3.00 points. Best Appearing Car award winners were Frame, Bill White, Garnant and Ted Simpson. Neatest Appearing Driver and Pit Crew awards went to Speed Hinkley, Quinn and Schurch.

Quinn opened the program by winning the two-lap "Helmet Dash." Cantlon was second and May, third. The "Victory Crown" presentation (and traditional kiss) was made by starlet Dorothy Ates.

Herman Schurch snared the 25-lap special event with Mel McKee, second, and Charley Gelston, third. Swede Smith blew a tire and smashed into the fence. He escaped with bruises.

The 100-lap main event offered more excitement as Quinn wove through heavy traffic to win, with the high-flying Triplett hounding him all the way to the checkered flag. Stubblefield was third, Brunmier, fourth. Bill Heisler, Walt May, Wilbur Shaw, Ryder, Bob Scovell, Chris Vest, Earl Hovenden and Merzney followed in that order.

Cycle events were won by Jacobs, who beat Briggs in the two-lap dash. Bigsby won the five-lap solo. Olson second and Bryant third.

For the March 23, 1930 racing show, James Vai replaced Milton as referee. Vai also became assistant steward under Dr. Loring, who became the new chief steward. Bill Claus returned as pit manager after Cliff Bergere went east to resume racing. Edward Pendleton replaced Roy E. Tuttle as chief timer. Walter Smith was instilled as auditor. Gasoline service was provided by U. S. Refining Co. The Legion executive board was unchanged.

For the racing program Bert Spencer returned in the "Chevrolet Special" after a brief absence. Other new driver entries were Paul Barrett, S-R "Fronty;" Curley Grandell, S-R "Fronty;" Jack Webb, "Rasor Special;" Charlie Cyr, "Lewis Special;" Fred Cooper, "Green Special."

Shorty Cantlon won the two-lap "Helmet Dash" in Bill White's Miller. Guy Deulin was second, Stubblefield, third. The time was 59.20. Grandell won a five-lap heat race, with Bob Scovell, second. Earl Hovenden, McKee, Petillo finish in that order in another five lapper. Hovenden repeated in a special five lapper. Grandell was second and Woody Woodford, third.

Stubblefield stole the thunder from Quinn in the 100-lap main event after grabbing the lead on the final lap. Deulin, Gelston, Phil Pardee and Harry Jacquez finished accordingly in 53 minutes, 16.80 seconds.

The race for the championship saw

Swede Smith take over first place with 114.02 points, followed by Quinn with 104.03, Walt May, "Stubby," Cantlon, Krieger, Ted Simpson, Triplett, Sharp, Frame and Harry Jacquez last with 1.04 points.

Quinn's "Dayton Thorobred Special," now driven by Speed Hinkley, was judged among the leading cars, along with those of Ryder, Pardee, Frame, Smith and Stubblefield's. Leading cars for Best Appearing Car honors were Frame, Simpson, Quinn, White, Grandell, Garnant and Paul Weirick. Race for Best Appearing Driver and Pit Crew awards found Quinn leading followed by Ryder, Phil Pardee, Frame, Stubblefield and Smith.

"Wee" Wilbur Shaw had arrived a few months earlier with the Johnny Vance "Red Pete" car out of Dayton, Ohio. The car had four carburetors, 16 valves and a double overhead camshaft, Frontenac heads on a Ford block with special rods. But the Vance car offered nothing but trouble for Shaw. A broken piston, a lost wheel, broken wrist pin, blown engines, broken front, then rear axle and Wilbur finally gave up. Shaw's luck didn't change until he drove for crafty Art Sparks, but even then had to wait 18 months for his first Ascot victory.

Ascot racked up another fatality on the night of October 15, 1930. Lynn Eldridge, a Pasadena leadfoot, was hurtled to instant death when he plowed into the back straighaway fence after his "Fronty" Ford blew a rear tire. The car burst into flames at impact.

By mid-1930, more movie stars had begun to fill Ascot's fancy loge section. Among them were Jack Oakie, Andy Devine, Vince Barnett, Carole Lombard and others. They joined such other stars as Charlie Chaplin, Bing Crosby, Clark Gable, Loretta Young and Doug Fairbanks Jr.

Realizing the popularity being generated at Ascot, producer Howard Hawks (through the stars' persuasion) chose Ascot as the site for an action-packed thriller, "The Crowd Roars." The movie starred James Cagney, Joan Blondell, supported by Ann Dvorak, Regis Toomey, Frank McHugh, Guy Kibbee and Eric Linden.

All of the action was filmed at Ascot, with the following drivers participating: Phil Pardee, "Stubby" Stubblefield, Wilbur Shaw, Quinn, Triplett, Babe Stapp and Ralph Hepburn. Stapp also assisted as technical director.

When the "action" switched briefly to Indianapolis, the Warner Brothers production featured such drivers as Shorty Cantlon, Billy Arnold, Fred Frame, Louie Schneider, Lou Moore and others.

Advertising billboards publicized the upcoming extravaganza thusly:

"Speed demons with goggled eyes glued on glory—grinning at death—laughing at love—breaking necks to break records while the crowd roars for blood. NEVER has the screen shown such nerve-shattering action lifted right off the track of the world's greatest speedway. It's the thrill epic of all time . . . the talk of every town that's seen it. Forty men risked death to film it . . . miss it at your own risk."

That was Ascot in 1930. A blend of death-defying racing, enormous enthusiastic and cheering crowds, "Victory Crown" presentations and a touching kiss from a motion picture starlet—the fans going wild with delight—flashy cars, American Legion Band music, stars in the stands and cameras grinding away at the action. And a high budget racing picture put more icing on the cake. What more could auto racing fans ask?

On December 4, 1930, death returned to Ascot. Boom! Crash! Kenny Morgan, a comparatively young driver and a newcomer to the speedway, was fatally injured in a fiery smashup on the home straightaway before a horrified capacity crowd. His car burst into flames seconds after he was pulled from the cockpit. Morgan had had limited experience, yet was tabbed "a comer."

Swede Smith, a Portlander, came out of nowhere to press Quinn and the "Big Six" for the 1930 title. Smith had amassed more than 100 points to lead the pack. However, late in the season he suddenly encountered trouble with Lloyd Vieux's "Vieux Special" speedster. Quinn, second place in the point standings for several weeks, wrested the lead and flashed to the 1930 championship. Quinn and Russ Garnant's "Gabhart Special" No. 2 were almost an unbeatable combination during the final weeks of the 1930 season.

Quinn was crowned champion at a special gathering at the race track and later at the Alexandria Hotel in Los Angeles. He accepted the Dick Dodd Memorial Championship Trophy, the Best Appearing Car and Crew Award, the annual Frank Verbeck award and the generous cash prize from the AAA Western Regional office. Car owner Russ Garnant and pit crewmen also attended the festivities, as did Quinn's racing opponents.

The 1930 championship season had been laid to rest. Dark depression days also prevailed but the fans, poor as many were, somehow found their way to Ascot. Apparently there was too much drama and excitement to keep them away.

Final standings for the 1930 Pacific Southwest Championship were:

1—Quinn. 2—Kenealy. 3—May. 4—Triplett. 5—Shaw. 6—Stubblefield. 7—Smith. 8—Brunmier. 9—Schurch. 10—Cantlon. 11—Hinkley. 12—Mckee. 13—Ryder. 14—Pardee.

Smith was in contention during more than half of the season, but lost ground when his "Vieux Special" started sputtering. Defending champ Kenealy closed fast and wound up second after a slow start. May finished a strong third in the "Multi-Ford" Frontenac. Shaw, despite troubles with the "Red Pete Special," got back into contention for a respected fifth place finish.

Ascot had lost none of its glory . . . there were more thrilling races on the horizon. The crowning of new champions, more spills, faster cars and the influx of new drivers, would be among the highlights of the future.

Francis Quinn receives trophies for winning 1930 Pacific Southwest championship. H. Kirby Shellaby, an AAA official, makes presentation. At the mike is Herb Marow. That's Pop Evans, background, wearing hat.

World's wrestling champion Ed "Strangler" Lewis visited the Ascot infield to chat with Francis Quinn on a Sunday afternoon in 1930. Lewis was a headliner in California rings and in the international mat world. Quinn, of course, was speed king at Ascot at that time.

They're off on another Ascot 100 lapper on June 7, 1931. Ernie Triplett takes the lead on the pole. Mel McKee is on the front row outside. Babe Stapp is behing Triplett. "Stubby" Stubblefield is in car No. 5. Francis Quinn is on the outside. Al Gordon is in Car No. 7. Beside Gordon is Johnny Krieger. Carl Ryder is on the outside.

Bob Carey is on the outside, Francis Quinn in the center and Ernie Triplett on the pole during this Ascot "Helmet Dash." Fred "Pop" Wagner waived the green "go-ahead" flag.

Francis Quinn takes checkered flag from a waiving Fred "Pop" Wagner during five-lap heat race. Billy Arnold finished second in this one.

Ascot Speedway on a Sunday afternoon. Note the symmetrical lines of hundreds of automobiles parked by enthusiastic auto racing fans.

This 1932 picture can rightfully be called "Ghosts of Ascot." Ernie Triplett sits in Bill White's "Red Lion Special" Miller. Ernie is flanked by AAA officials, including Art Pillsbury kneeling at left. Car crew members are Ed Wintergust, Eddie Offut and Dale Drake. Superimposed, standing, from left are Mel Kenealy, Kelly Petillo, Sam Palmer and Babe Stapp. Kneeling, from left, are Wilbur Shaw (crash helmet), Triplett himself, Al Gordon, Chet Gardner and Phil Pardee. (Doug Boyd collection.)

Danny De Paulo, car owner, and driver Phil Pardee in the "Gilmore Lion Special," a 191 cubic inch Miller.

Ernie Triplett, who once again won the Victory Crown. That's Peggy Hamilton doing the honors.

Art Pillsbury, Western Region AAA director, shakes the hand of diminutive "Wee Wilbur" Shaw after one of his many victories. The Blue-Green Special was a 220 cu. in, Miller.

Pretty actress Jeanne Dunn presents Ernie Triplett with the Victory Crown helmet after a "Helmet Dash" win, one of many for famed Ernie. That's Bill White's Miller.

A couple of "Wild Bills" of the Cummings family. Young "Wild Bill" (left) was a very colorful and spectacular driver at Ascot. Dad Cummings was a prominent driver on Texas and Arizona tracks from 1910 to 1920.

Dick Doyle, the tire changer, right, held the world record of 8¾ seconds for the feat. Here he shows "Shorty" Cantlon, left, and Johnny Kreiger, Ascot drivers, how he does it. December 15, 1930.

Babe Stapp was seriously injured in an April 1932 race at Ascot, but returned in August for a 100 lapper at the famed Legion-sponsored speedway. Ace mechanic Russ Garnant gives the Babe some pointers.

Actress Gilda Grey presents Carl Ryder with victory cup . . . a money prize came later from racing officials. Ryder won a 5-lap heat during that 1930 evening.

Gilmore Racing Team, 1932. From left: Wilbur Shaw, Arvol Brunmier, Lester Spangler, "Stubby" Stubblefield, "Will Bill" Cummings and Howdy Wilcox. They drove the finest cars of the day.

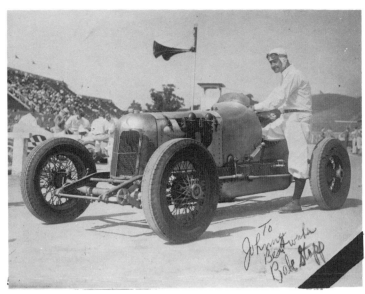

Ready to qualify. Babe Stapp, clad in nickers, steps into Francis Quinn's Miller Marine 91 cubic inch job. Francis later boosted displacement to 244. It's a 1930 race day.

The irrepressible Speed Hinkley. The car a Miller Marine, was built by Francis Quinn. It's qualifying time for a 1930 race.

"Wee Wilber" Shaw, a resplendent looking driver on March 8, 1932, the first driver ever to wear a crash helmet on an American auto racing track. Shaw was fastest qualifier this day but bowed to "Wild Bill" Cummings in a scorching 100-lap main event.

hil Pardee in the "Simpson Special" on August 24, 1929. Ted impson's car was a 12-cylinder Chrysler which attracted atten-on at Ascot.

Ascot driver Bob Hahn in the "American Special." Hahn was killed in the 1932 Indianapolis race while riding as mechanic for Pete Kreis, who also died. Leo Munson stands alongside. Man, right, unidentified.

A little warming up and jocking for position before full acceleration at the starting line. Front, on pole, is Mel Kenealy. On outside is Bill Spence (99). Second row, on pole, is Babe Stapp, with "Stubby" Stubblefield on the outside. Behind Stubby is Francis Quinn. Bill Cummings is alongside Quinn. Kelly Petillo is at the rear. It's race day, 1929.

Blasting out of the south turn is the leader Ernie Triplett during a November 8, 1931, main event. Car owner Bill White later changed the numeral 4 to numeral 1 for Ernie's championship that year. Trailing the "Blond Terror" are Bryan Saulspaugh, Bill Cummings, Herman Schurch, Wilbur Shaw, Chet Gardner, Johnny Kreiger and Babe Stapp.

Thunder on the Ascot main straightaway, 1932. On the pole, front row, is Bill Cummings. On the outside is Les Spangler. Behind Cummings is Bob Carey, with Kelly Petillo on the outside. In the third row are Arvol Brunmier (inside) and Mel McKee. Ernie Triplett is on the inside, fourth row, with Sam Palmer on outside.
(Courtesy Roscoe Turner.)

Ascot greats take slow warmup at start of 150-lap, 12-car main event, 1932. Mel Kenealy has the pole in Earl Haskell's No. 18 Miller. Champion Ernie Triplett is on the outside in Bill White's "Red Lion Special" No. 1. Second row is Sam Palmer and Chet Gardner (No. 2) on the outside. Kelly Petillo is on the pole, third row, with Wilbur Shaw on outside. Babe Stapp is in the fourth row, inside, and Les Spangler on outside. Fifth row has Mel McKee (inside) and Herman Schurch on outside. On the pole in last row is Carl Ryder. Louie Tomei is on the outside. Is there an empty seat in the stands?

Screw on the loose. Ernie Triplett appears oblivious to loosened and flapping cowling as he steams into the south turn in the Bill White Miller, It's 1931 . . . a championship is in the making.

Ascot action coming out of south turn. Unidentified cars at speed.
(Courtesy Roscoe Turner.)

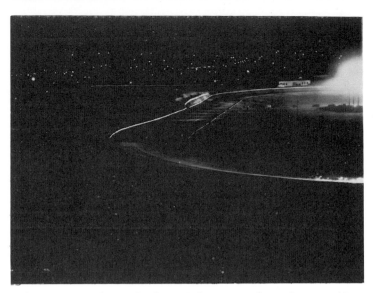

Night view of Ascot's back straightaway and north turn. Note string of lights along back stretch fence. This helped the drivers to "pick up" the back straightaway as they zoomed out of the south turn. ......
(Courtesy Roscoe Turner.)

Rex Mays bounced off the south turn fence as Ernie Triplett whizzed by in the No. 1 "Red Lion Special." Mays escaped injury during this "Helmet Dash" encounter with the 1931-32 Coast Champion. Mays' car is the "Hispano Special" aircraft motor powered speedster.

Ascot action, 1932. Chet Gardner (No. 2 "Miller Special") goes high on the south turn. Wilbur Shaw, wearing the first crash helmet on an American track, drives the No. 28 "Mallory Special" between the cars. Wildman Carl Ryder spins out of control in No. 9.
(Courtesy Roscoe Turner.)

Shorty Cantlon raises hand, a motion for the boys to line up for start of a 1931 "Helmet Dash." Behind Shorty is Bob Carey. Bill Cummings is in Art Sparks' No. 6 Miller. Cantlon tools the No. 10 "Lion Head Special."
(Doug Boyd collection.)

"Stubby" Stubblefield in Harlan Fengler's "Cragar Special" in 1931. "Stubby" was killed qualifying for the 1935 Indianapolis race. Fengler later became chief steward at Indy. Stubblefield drove the Cragar impressively at Ascot.

Wilbur Shaw brought Johnny Vance's "Red Pete" car to Ascot in 1930. The 16-valve job hailed from Dayton, Ohio, but Shaw was beset by a steady barrage of mechanical woes. "Wee Wilbur" never did get the bugs out of this one.

Roland Frost, a driver as well as car owner. Here he is on March 31, 1931.

"Shorty" Cantlon in the "Lion Head Special!" No. 10. Mel Kenealy also drove this car. December 10, 1932.

"Midwest Cyclone" Bryan Saulspaugh in the "Gilmore Red Lion Special" at Ascot in 1933. The car was driven by Les Spangler that year for finishing second in 1932 point standings. Saulspaugh was killed in a two-man car race at Oakland's mile speedway. Incidentally, the little boy (arrow) standing beside the post is your author. Would you believe it? A three-year "Ascot veteran" at that age!

Pals of the roaring road . . . when they're off the track, that is. From left are "Stubby" Stubblefield, Arvol Brunmier, Ernie Triplett and Francis Quinn. Quinn was the reigning champ, Triplett was coming on strong, Arvol had set the night one-lap record and "Stubby" gave everybody pure heck.

You guys gettin' enough traction? Harry Schmidt (center), Ascot track superintendent, discusses and examines Ascot's speedy dirt-oil racing surface with "Stubby" Stubblefield, left, and Wilbur Shaw (Courtesy Roscoe Turner.)

Blanche Mehaffey presents Victory Crown. Carl Ryder has that pensive, but perhaps happy look, after 1931 "Italian Helmet Dash" win. (Courtesy Roscoe Turner.)

"Babe" Stapp receives an affectionate kiss from an unindentified little girl for winning the "Helmet Dash" in Chad McClurg's big Miller "Gilmore Speedway Special." The triplets are John, Howard and Bill Hertel of Glendale.

Intrepid trio. Arvol Brunmier, left; Bill Cummings, center, Francis Quinn, right. Ascot favorites display Mohawk tires.
(Courtesy Roscoe Turner.)

Wooden tiers divide Ascot car pits, but mechanics had plenty of room to work on cars. It's a 1933 race day. Car No. 28 is Tommy Newton's. Car No. 6 is National champ Bob Carey's. Car No. 4 (foreground) is Chet Gardner's "Miller Special." Car No. 26 is the "Zotterelli Special" driven by Louis Tomei.

The last picture taken of 1932 National AAA champion Bob Carey. It is April 16, 1933, at Legion Ascot Speedway, moments before Carey's fatal accident on the north turn. It was a Saturday "practice day." The car is the Joe Marks "Lion Head Special."

Smashed . . . bent . . . a life snuffed out. National AAA champ Bob Carey's fatal wreck in the Joe Marks' "Lion Head Special" of Gary, Indiana. It was a dismal day at Ascot on April 16, 1933. Carey was warming car for Easter Sunday race when wreck occurred.

Another view of Kenny Stoddard's fatal wreck on Ascot's dangerous south turn. The ill-fated driver can be seen at the extreme right. Despite thrilling races, the spectre of the Grim Reaper took no holiday in this 1928 wreck.   (Doug Boyd collection.)

Kenny Stoddard took a nasty spill . . . with fatal results . . . in this December 22, 1928 Ascot mishap on the south turn. Broken front wheel, another sheered off wheel and other car parts are strewn on the fatal south turn. Stoddard lies motionless at left. Driver at left unidentified.
     (Doug Boyd collection.)

Frank Suess met the Grim Reaper in this two-car smashup on Ascot's main straightaway on June 14, 1933. Suess' car locked wheels with car driven by French La Horgue (background). La Horgue was seriously injured. Ted Horn suffered minor injuries in this 15-lap consolation race.

Frank Suess, killed at Ascot, 1933. His career didn't last too long, Suess gave his utmost in trying to establish himself as a racing driver. Injuries in a two-car wreck on the main straightaway were fatal.

George Young was the 9th ranking driver during 1930. But a terrific four-car pile-up on the north turn ended his bid for the championship. Young hailed from Milwaukee, Wisconsin.

George Young fatal wreck, Ascot Speedway, 1930. Young's car is seen over the fence resting on its side and up against the protective wire fencing just outside the north turn. Foreground is Lester Spangler (pushing his car away from the fence). At left is car No. 8, driven by Arvol Brunmier. Not seen (over the fence to right) is car driven by Curley Grandell. Spangler, Brunmier and Grandell escaped injury.

Sam Palmer, the "miracle man" of racing. The plucky Los Angeles pilot one day skidded more than 100 feet down the main straightaway before 10,000 horrified fans. Sam escaped disaster and was soon back in the driver's cockpit.

Here's how Sam Palmer's car ended up after his 100-foot up-side-down skid on the main straightaway on March 31, 1933. Sam was only bumped and bruised.

The gruesome remains of which once was a racing car, the fatal wreck of H.D. (Hal) Provan at Ascot on November 20, 1933. The car had burst into flames at impact with a hillside outside the back straightaway.

H.D. (Hal) Provan was a young and aspiring driver until the night of November 20, 1933, when his "Y Service Special" shot out of control on the back stretch and plunged over the fence. The accident occurred during a 10-lap consolation race. This is the last picture taken of Provan, minutes before going onto the track for the last time.

Wreck of the "Bullock Boring Service Special" in February, 1931. Car blasted the north turn fence and plowed into field. Accident resulted in the death of Tom Forsythe.

For Lynn Eldrige it was a final ride after he flipped in the north turn while warming his car on April 2, 1930. A blown tire did him in. Note how car dug itself into the track surface.

Bob Austin cheated death in this accident out of the north turn in 1934. Austin sailed through the protective fence and took some with him, as depicted.

Earl Farmer of Inglewood, California, struck and catapulted over the south turn fence and rolled several times, ending up against the outside wire fencing. His injuries were fatal in the "Inglewood Special" during this dismal February 2, 1931 day.

Zipping out of the north turn in 1930. Bill Cummings leads, with Wilbur Shaw in the Johnny Vance "Red Pete Special" on the inside. Babe Stapp is at "Wild Bill's" tail. Francis Quinn is high on turn ready to make a move.

Nice view of Legion Ascot Speedway looking toward the north turn and part of the main straightaway. (Courtesy Roscoe Turner.)

Rex Mays poses with E.J. "Sandy" Sanders of the Gilmore Oil Co. Paul Fromm had his Model-B sparkling with new paint when this 1934 picture was taken.

Chet Gardner and his big "Miller Special." Chet died at Flemingron, N.J., in 1938, when he chose to strike the fence to avoid a young boy who ran onto the track.

Clyde Bloomgren in the "Pop-Eye Special" No. 54, Ascot Speedway, 1932.

Bill Cummings hot-lapped this "Miller Special" many times in 1932. He also drove for Art Sparks sparingly during the 1933 season before returning to the National circuit, eventually winning the Indy 500 in 1934.

The "Arnold Special" was a Miller rocket owned by 1930 Indianapolis winner Billy Arnold. Intrepid Ernie Triplett took it for a spin at Ascot on this 1930 day.

Rex Mays in the "Hispano (Hisso) Special" at Legion Ascot Speedway, 1933.
(Photo courtesy Mrs. Rex (Dorothy) Mays, Santa Ana, California.)

Carl Ryder in Doug Harrison's (standing) "Gilmore Special." Ryder was an Ascot attraction for many years. September 4, 1932.

"Miller Schofield Special" was the first disc-wheeled car ever driven at Ascot. Bill White, owner, right, and driver Shorty Cantlon admire the Miller creation. Man, left, unidentified. That's Woody Woodford, with helmet on, at rear. It's 1930.

Frank Witty in the "Denver Special." It was a Saturday afternoon, August 26, 1931, practice day at Ascot. Everybody was admitted free, naturally.

Johnny Kreiger in Charlie Caraba's "Western Super Special," November 10, 1929.

Chet Gardner, "Miller Special" at Legion Ascot Speedway, 1931.

Walt May in the "Tri-Flex Special," Ascot, 1931. His last victory before being fatally injured at San Jose's 5/8 mi. track.

The nervy, skillful Jimmy Sharp in the Sharp was killed on the Oakland mile

(above) **An eagle and a thorobred. That's "Bald Eagle" Francis Quinn behind the wheel of the "Dayton Thorobred Special" 191 cubic inch Miller, in which he drove to the 1930 Pacific Southwest championship. Quinn would switch from this car to the Fronty Ford "Gabhart Special" enroute to the title. Note the down draft carburetor. That's brother Les Quinn, far right.**

Joe Crocker was a mechanic and at times an enthusiastic driver. It's 1929. The car is Bill Heisler's "Fronty Special," a single cam S-R Fronty, on a Model-T Ford block.

(below) **Bill Spence pulls in front of stands after winning the "Helmet Dash" on March 13, 1927. Spence, a strong competitor at Ascot, made a bold bid to win the 1929 Indianapolis race, but was killed in that Memorial Day event which was won by Ray Keech.**

The car in which Bill "Re California, one mile dirt tr cial" at Ascot in 1929.

ey Special" in 1930, Ascot Speedway.
n 1932, that track's first fatality.

Tony Radetich in the "Dugan Special." He was 13th ranking driver for 1929 at Ascot Speedway. A unique car, for sure. Bob Mandic stands (center).

(above) The Fronty Ford "McDowell Special" which provided plenty of thrills with hell-bent-for-leather driver Charles Gelston at the throttle. Gelston was one of many dirt track devils who came to Ascot in 1925. Charley carries the Numeral 1, a champion elsewhere, perhaps, because Ascot did not crown a champ prior to 1928.

(below) Eastern campaigner Lou Moore brought his classy "Frost Miller Special" to Ascot in 1927. Years later, Moore gained fame as builder of the "Blue Crown Specials" in which Mauri Rose, Bill Holland and George Conners drove at Indianapolis.

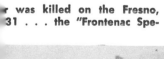

was killed on the Fresno,
31 . . . the "Frontenac Spe-

Herb Balmer lived in Eagle Rock and constantly made the trip to drive at Ascot. Herb lost his life in that community when he took to a hillside to test a stock racer. On the track, though, Herb was a stick-out driver.

Bill Heisler lived in Hawthorne, California, and was one of Ascot's best drivers. A crash on the Bakersfield mile track ended his life. At Ascot, he drove the "Heisler Special," the car in which he was killed.

Ernie Triplett, when he was the 1931 Pacific Coast big-car AAA champion.

Mauri Rose came from the midwest where he faced the top dirt track drivers for years. He drove at Ascot and later restricted himself to Indianapolis events, winning three times, (1941-47-48).

Jimmy Sharp was killed Nov. 1, 1931, when his car bolted through a guardrail and went over a 15-foot bank at Oakland Speedway during a 100-mile AAA event. The Los Angeles driver was a close contender for the Pacific Southwest championship at the time of the accident.

A candid shot of "Whittier Shiek" Arvol Brunmier, one of Ascot's all-time standouts.

"Speed" Hinckley, who was among the pilots to enter the annual July 4, 1928, racing program as promoted by American Legion, Post 127.

Chet Gardner, the "old man of the mountain." Chet was known as a money driver. You could find him among the leaders at the finish in many races.

Howdy Wilcox, on Nov. 21, 1932. An outstanding competitor at Ascot who later became famous on the National circuit.

Wilbur Shaw, 1937-39-40 Indianapolis winner, poses with first crash helmet ever worn by a driver in competition on a U.S. track (Ascot, 1932). The helmet, made mandatory for all drivers in 1934, was a gift from Major H.O.D. Segrave of England; spring, 1932.

George Young of Milwaukee, Wisconsin, who was killed on Ascot's north turn during a four-car pileup in 1931. The wreck also involved Curley Grandell, Arvol Brunmier and Lester Spangler.

Art Boyce, the "old ambulance driver" who gave the boys plenty of headaches at the old Alhambra area oval. Boyce was a leading contender in the opening of the 1933 season and was always a threat. In 1934, Boyce flipped on the back straightaway and he too had to be carted away in an ambulance.

Francis Quinn in the "Gabhart Special" Fronty Ford in which he won the 1930 Pacific Southwest championship. Russ Garnant of Glendale, California, was the car's chief mechanic.

Francis Quinn and Arvol Brunmier were pals off the Ascot speed-paths. But once on it, all friendship was forgotten. Electrifying were their speed duels, week after week.

The "Ballanger Rajo" was a fast little Fronty Ford chariot which Francis Quinn drove to its limit during the mid-twenties at Ascot. Cecil Ballanger was owner of the car. Note ropes tied to rear and front axles to minimize vibration.

In 1929, Francis Quinn drove the "Schmidt Special" Miller with fair success. He switched later to the Dayton Thorobred and Gabhart cars on way to the championship.

Francis Quinn receives good luck handshake before setting onto the Ascot track for a fast practice lap or two. Quinn's brother Les stands at the right of the "Bald Eagle."

Board track star and veteran Indianapolis driver Harry Hartz gets a "feel" of Francis Quinn's "Dayton Thorobred Special." It's March 1930, just prior to Quinn qualifying.

Autograph time. Al Gordon pencils his "John Henry" on a checkered flag for an Ascot official. A nice memento for some lucky person.

A most familiar scene . . . Ernie Triplett winning the "Helmet Dash." Will the motion picture industry please tell us who this beautiful young lady is.

Ernie Triplett, left, and Francis Quinn. Two of the most bitter rivals in the history of auto racing.   (Courtesy Al and Gertrude Dorcey.)

It's the end of the 1931 racing season. Veteran starter Fred "Pop" Wagner presents second place trophy to Chet Gardner. Ernie Triplett, rear, had received the championship trophy.

Stagecoach drivers? Nope. Nick Martino, Arvol Brunmier and Francis Quinn celebrated La Fiesta Night in recognition of Los Angeles' 150th birthday on September 9, 1930. The racing card was billed La Fiesta Sweepstakes. Speed Hinkley is in the cockpit.

Lineup of drivers and officials in 1931. Standing in back row are George Conners, Bill Heisler, Pat Cunningham, Al Gordon, Speed Hinkley, Charles Gelston, Fred Merzney, Art Boyce, Harry Hartz, Fred Wagner and others. Kneeling are Phil Pardee, Tommy Cosman, Woody Woodford, Jimmy Sharp, "Stubby" Stubblefield, Ernie Triplett, Arvol Brunmier, Mel Kenealy, Art Pillsbury, among others.

Francis Quinn skips along in the Bellanger Rajo during night race at Ascot. Bill Spence rides the inside in second place.

One of the first pictures taken of Rex Mays at Ascot . . . 1931. Rex is young and ambitious at the wheel of the "Mays Special." The car is Willie Utzman's Winfield Model-A Flathead. Jack and Fred Rand were owners of the car.
(Courtesy Mrs. Rex Mays, of Santa Ana, California).

Christening a new "Miller Special" is Gertrude Allen in this 1931 picture. Francis Quinn, 1930 Southwest champ, is at left. Quinn's close friend and bitter rival Walt May is at right. Quinn's creation cost $6,000, quite a bit of money during those depression days...

"Shorty" Cantlon in Bill White's "Miller Schofield Special," the first rear disc-wheeled car driven at Ascot. April 14, 1930. It was the world's fastest four-cylinder car.

One of the greatest of women swimmers Eleanor Holm and USC Trojan football great Ray Sparling chat with Ernie Triplett on September 13, 1932, just before the Coast champ qualified for a night race. Triplett won the Helmet Dash and main event.

Swede Smith, 1933 Class-B champion, left, and Al Gordon, 1933 Class-A champ. Smith was killed at El Centro in 1934, Gordon died at Ascot in 1936. (Courtesy Roscoe Turner.)

Buddies on and off the track are left to right: Walt May, Ernie Triplett and Stubby Stubblefield. All Ascot veterans, but they all died on other tracks; May at San Jose, Triplett at El Centro, and Stubblefield at Indianapolis.

"Now boys, give the fans their money's worth." Could these have been the words of Dr. Fred Loring, head of the American Legion's Contest Board, just before a Wednesday night main event? Listening approvingly are Ernie Triplett, right, and Wilbur Shaw, who wears the first crash helmet ever worn on an American track.

Mel McKee, of Kansas, who raced Wilbur Shaw in a special five-lap match race, losing to "Wee" Wilbur in a wheel-to-wheel battle, 1932.

Charles Heisler didn't win many races at Ascot, but he was always in competition, either on a Sunday or Wednesday night. Feb. 11, 1933.

"Blond Terror" Ernie Triplett in 1931. No better driver ever appeared at the American Legion promoted race track.

"Shorty" Cantlon, on May 3, 1930, 28 days before his second place finish (behing Billy Arnold) in the Indy 500. Cantlon drove cars in a highly reckless fashion around the Legion Ascot Speedway track.

"Wild Bill Cummings," who won many thrilling races at Ascot. Bill also won the 1934 Indianapolis race. Cummings was among the all-time Ascot favorites who provided plenty of "heat" for his rivals.

Cloth helmeted Wilbur Shaw smiles confidently before the start of the Italian Helmet Dash on Feb. 6, 1932. A few months later, Shaw set a precedent as Ascot—becoming the first driver to wear a crash helmet on an American track.

The great Francis Quinn, Pacific Southwest Champion, 1930. "Dayton Thorobred Special" No. 8. Joe Gemsa of El Monte, California, at one time owned the car. Gemsa also possessed the Dick Dodd Trophy (depicted), courtesy of Les Quinn — Francis's brother.

Earl B. Gilmore, who sponsored many sparkling "Gilmore Special" racing cars at Ascot. His company (Gilmore Oil Company) sponsorship assisted tremendously in putting Ascot on a high plain in auto racing.
(Courtesy Roscoe Turner.)

"Stubby" Stubblefield was a kindly guy from South Gate, California, as well as a great little driver. He held back for no one. But one day, while practicing at Indianapolis, "Stubby" took his last ride in 1935.

"Shorty" Cantlon, December 8, 1931. The little Detroit pilot used to sit on cushions to peer over the cockpit.

Entrance into Ascot Speedway parking grounds, off Valley Boulevard. It's 1932 . . . and a bit hazy (is it smog?) . . . would you believe it!

Mel Kenealy in the "Maes Special" No. 7 barely gets by a spinning Sam Palmer, car No. 9. Action is on south turn, 1932.

View of grandstand along main straightaway as Ascot, 1930.

(Courtesy Roscoe Turner.)

Arvol Brunmier in Harvey Ward's No. 5 Miller leads Bill Cummings in Danny DePaolo's No. 19 Miller. Arvol was too hot to handle that day, September 18, 1932.

Shorty Cantlon was a gutty and talented driver from Detroit, Michigan, who arrived at Ascot in 1929. Winning "Helmet Dash" honors this 1930 day were his. Cantlon died in a smashup in the 1947 Indianapolis race.

Nick Martino in Harvey Ward's "Gilmore Speedway Special," 1932. But who's the gal? In this car, Arvol Brunmier set the all-time night lap record of 25.92 seconds.

Ernie Triplett in Bill White's Miller powered car, 1931. Triplett, fourth ranking driver the year before, drove this car to successive titles, 1931-32, and carried the numeral 1 through 1933.

American League slugger Jimmy Foxx congratulates Jimmy Sharp after a main event win in the "Gabhart Special." Sharp was driving Russ Garnant's car to the 1930 title but he was injured later on the Bakersfield mile. Sharp come back too soon, and was killed on the Oakland Mile, 1931. Francis Quinn then drove car to the title.

et's race," a smiling Rex Mays seems to say. The Riverside aredevil is in Ed Winfield's Model-B bullet.

Francis Quinn wins another "Italian Helmet Dash" in the Dayton Thorobred Special." The woman who presented Quinn the Victory Crown is unidentified.

Ernie Triplett wins another "Helmet Dash." Who's the starlet with the Clara Bow-style hat? We know the car is Barney Kleopfer's "Barney Special" Fronty. The year: 1929.
(Doug Boyd Collection.)

Woody Woodford, who first appeared at Ascot in 1928. A tough customer all the way.

A young, (1930) smiling and energetic Norman J. Hartford was Ascot's publicity writer who wrote weekly columns in programs which sold for 15 cents. Hartford would also broadcast Ascot races over radio KGFJ. Hartford died in Santa Ana, California, in 1974, after years of wrestling, boxing and auto racing publicity writing. He was a highly talented man who created the Francis Quinn-Ernie Triplett "feud."

Frenchy La Horgue, popular Ascot driver who was involved in Frank Suess's fatal wreck on the home stretch.

Herb Balmer is congratulated after a May 1, 1933, consolation win at Ascot. Who's the well-wisher? Does anybody know?

Bill Koller who relieved the aging Fred "Pop" Wagner as starter at the Legion Ascot Speedway. Koller was chief starter until the track's closure.   (Courtesy Roscoe Turner.)

Car builder Russ Garnant works in his Glendale machine shop in 1931. The car is a DO Miller-Schofield on a stock Model-A Ford block, later called a DO Cragar.   (Doug Boyd collection.)

Ascot favorites Les Spangler, left, and Babe Stapp pose with a friend—Miss Martha Cox, on August 1, 1932.

CHAPTER IV

THE "BLOND TERROR"

(1931 - 1933)

❧

The name, Ernie Triplett, is as synonymous with Ascot history as Charles Lindbergh's is with aviation.

Triplett, who was known as the "Blond Terror" and the "Belvedere Badboy" for his aggressive, nerveless and refined driving ability, was in a class by himself during the 1931 season at the American Legion Speedway and on other tracks of the West Coast and Southwestern states. Triplett won the 1931 Pacific Southwest championship and repeated in 1932, thus becoming the first driver to win two successive titles. It was during the 1931-32 racing seasons when Ascot would reach its zenith in popularity. Gate receipts of $5,000 would soon swell to $15,000 per show.

So dominant was lanky Triplett during the two campaigns, especially in 1931, he was the scourge of Ascot, and other drivers, although pushing him to the limit, were often considered "also-rans." The "Blond Terror" was practically unbeatable.

It was with justification and sound reasoning that ace mechanic and car builder Paul Weirick once stated, "There was no better driver than Ernie Triplett."

The 1931 season unfolded with a full-house of 12,000 to witness a 100-lap main event on New Year's Day. However, the new year offered more grief when another driver was killed. This time it was youthful Earl Farmer.

During the main event Farmer accelerated too fast going into the south turn, skidded about 75 feet, then another 50 feet before skyrocketing over the fence and down the embankment. The "Fronty" Ford's left front tire had blown, causing the accident. Triplett flashed to the main event win. But the fans were stunned over Farmer's fatal crash.

During 1931 five drivers gave Triplett lots of competition, however. They were Arvol Brunmier, "Wild Bill" Cummings,

Chet Gardner, Lester Spangler and "Stubby" Stubblefield. Very capable men, but they just couldn't match Ernie's natural ability. At this time, 1930 champion Francis Quinn was experiencing difficulty (he was troubled all year) in getting the "bugs" out of his new $6,000 Miller, the gold No. 1 "Francis Quinn Special." Quinn had built the pale blue beauty with his championship earnings. Unlike the 1930 season, 1931 was not to be his.

The 1931 season also saw many other drivers behind the wheel of speedy Miller powered racing cars. Brunmier drove the "Piston Ring Shop Special" No. 48, a car whose engine he called a "Miller Marine," for its design for speedboat racing. The motor was later installed in Arvol's race car chassis with reasonable success. Brunmier switched later to Art Sparks' more refined No. 6 "Miller Special." Stubblefield piloted the No. 3 "Cragar Special." Spangler drove the No. 69 "Montrose Special." Gardner tooled his huge 8-cylinder "Miller Special" No. 47. Cummings was the exception and stuck with the "Fronty Special" No. 19. At this time seat belts were not mandatory, their use was left to driver discretion.

When Triplett emerged upon the Ascot scene in 1926, after a brief apprenticeship at Banning Speedway, he was strictly a "Fronty" Ford driver. Intrepid Ernie drove these cars to the hilt. One was Barney Kleopfer's No. 33 "Barney Special." It was in 1929 when Triplett graduated to a more "class" car and drove Billy Arnold's fast No. 40 Miller, in which he hit his stride while dueling the great Quinn.

Triplett also drove the "Allen Special" No. 6 Miller during 1930 and in early 1931. Then his luck took another upswing when he was offered to drive the late W. S. (Bill) White's new race car—a "Miller Special" No. 4.

It was White who had introduced the first rear disc-wheeled car at Ascot in 1930, with Shorty Cantlon the driver. Meanwhile, White had persuaded Dale Drake, Eddie Offutt and Clyde Adams to build the new four-cylinder Miller, which was to become a gem of a racer. (Drake is the late Dale Drake of the famous Meyer-Drake Offenhauser engineering firm, for years producers of "Offy" engines) .White's new car was powered by a 220 cubic inch Miller motor with a special cylinder block.

The car debuted at the new Oakland mile oval in January, 1931, with Quinn behind the wheel. The new car, unpainted and under test, still had the "bugs" (as most all new cars have) and was not an immediate success. Quinn, busily trying to perfect his own new car, suggested to White that he get another driver.

White stuck to the old racing code: "When you have the best car, get the best driver." It was then that White got Triplett behind the wheel. Triplett would more than fulfill the driving assignment, as future events would show. After a bright red paint job and white No. 4, the new Miller became a beauty . . . hot stuff which made the fans gasp with envy. Triplett was destined to blaze to high-speed glory at Oakland, Ascot, San Jose and on other western tracks.

Farmer's death on January 1; the introduction of White's new Miller; Triplett's fast start towards winning the championship; were early highlights of the 1931 season. Yet, the spectre of the "Grim Reaper" was to make another awesome appearance. The shattering death of George Young on January 25, shook the populace.

Young, a heavy-footed Milwaukee driver, got tangled with Brunmier, Curley Grandell and Spangler during a five-lap heat race. Young tried to pass the leader, Spangler, coming out of the north turn, but

smashed against the fence and plowed through a 12-foot wire screen which had been erected to protect the spectators along the main straightaway. Grandell's car hit the north turn fence. He escaped unhurt. Brunmier's car flipped 25 feet into the air and landed on its wheels, the car's frame bent drastically. Brunmier, stunned, climbed instinctively from the car and wobbled along the track towards his crewmen. Young was decapitated. Spangler won the short race . . . it didn't matter . . . Young was dead.

Meanwhile, Triplett was having trouble with White's Miller speedster. The car got great torque power from its Miller motor, but the chassis wasn't handling properly. Drake and Eddie Offutt then installed cross springs on the car instead of the conventional side springs. The change was made as requested by Eddie Meyer to Bill White. (Meyer had introduced cross springs at Ascot as early as 1924) .

The changeover made a big difference. Triplett won 13 of the first 18 main events in which he drove at Ascot during 1931. Aside from these victories, some of which were 100 and 150-lap mains, Ernie also won many "Helmet Dashes" and heat races. He was unmatched. Many a Sunday afternoon and Wednesday night the fans would see Triplett receiving the victory kiss from a movie starlet for winning the ear-mashing helmet. Ernie's victory string became the talk of the track. Ascot was his!

Triplett accepted and fought off the challenges of all rivals; Spangler, Babe Stapp, Cummings, Brunmier, 1929 champ Mel Kenealy, Grandell, Walt May, Stubblefield, the hard-lucked Quinn and others couldn't stay with the hard driving "Blond Terror." Triplett's standout rivals also drove fast Miller cars, but to no avail. (Note: today's Drake Offenhauser motor is the "son" of the Miller motor. Harry Miller first built an eight-cylinder Miller for speedboat racing in 1919. Miller installed that same motor, known as the Miller Marine, into a racing car in 1924 for the late Jimmy Murphy. Without Miller's genius (with help from chief designer Leo Gossen) there never would have been an "Offy", because today's four banger is similar in design to the old Miller. Fred Offenhauser, a Miller engineer, took over the plant when Miller died and changed the motor patent to "Offenhauser." Miller, however, was the creator of that famous engine).

Meanwhile, Triplett was pocketing thousands of dollars on his victory splurge en route to the 1931 Southwest title in White's bright red, white numeraled Miller racer. The number 4 was really hot. Triplett won the first 100 miler at the new Oakland mile in the car, also pulled off victories at El Centro, San Jose, Bakersfield and Phoenix.

A race was scheduled on June 21, 1931, at the speedy five-eighth's mile track at San Jose. All of Ascot's finest-Triplett, Quinn, Spangler, Stapp, Stubblefield, Brunmier, Cummings and Walt May were entered. May, without a car to drive and leading the point standings, asked if he could drive Vic Felt's "Triflex Special" which was granted. Coming out of the fourth turn on his first lap, May hit a dirt embankment on the inside of the track, rolled it twice and went down the straighaway end over end. His feet got hooked in the steering wheel and that was it. May was a close friend of Quinn and Triplett. He was to be missed by the entire West Coast racing fraternity.

By November 1, Triplett had cinched the 1931 crown due to his wide margin of 300 points over second place Chet Gardner. The "Blond Terror" had beaten fine drivers in the likes of Stubblefield, who would finish third in the final standings. Trailing were Quinn, Brunmier, Les Spangler, Babe

Stapp, Cummings, Kenealy, Kelly Petillo, Cantlon, Phil Pardee, Wilbur Shaw, Speed Hinkley and Herman Schurch. Thirtieth on the list was youthful newcomer Rex Mays, who drove his own "Mays Special" No. 71. Four notches below was another novice—Ted Horn, with 39.74 points.

Horn arrived at Ascot in 1928, but he was seriously injured that year on the south turn where he tangled with Ted Simpson during a heat race. Horn was shelved, and forgotten, until the 1931 season while his injuries healed.

Mays came along in late 1931, after a brief campaign in his native Riverside, California. Mays worked on his uncle's fruit orchard and would whiz around the farm in a hopped-up Model-T truck. Bitten by the "speed bug," Rex later drove at Colton and at San Bernardino and eventually brought his hopped-up Ford to Ascot. Rex didn't do too much at the beginning, being barely 19 years old. But Lady Luck would point her finger in his direction, and Rex would become one of Ascot's all-time greats.

On November 7 another driver was killed at Ascot. Herman Schurch crashed to his death, adding another victim to Ascot's now infamous "caretaker list." Schurch, riding in fourth place behind Triplett, Brunmier and Spangler during a 100-lap main event, tried to pass Brunmier. His car careened out of control, vaulted over the south turn fence and went into another fatal roll down the embankment. "Who will be next?" a disgruntled fan was heard to grumble.

The 1931 Pacific Southwest championship was Triplett's. All the other drivers congratulated him for his one-sided victory, maintained their competitive spirit by saying, "Wait until next season . . . we'll get ya." And "Bald Eagle" Francis Quinn vowed to work on his new Miller during

123

the off-season and give Triplett a run for the 1932 championship. It was not to be.

To close the Southwest racing season, a 100-lap race was scheduled for December 14, 1931, at Oakland. The new oval was considered to be the most perfectly designed and fastest mile track on the National AAA circuit. All of Ascot's finest were entered. Many eastern AAA drivers such as Mauri Rose, Ralph Hepburn, Louie Meyer and others also were penned in the big sweepstakes. A full capacity crowd of 15,000 was expected.

Confident that his new Miller No. 1 was ready after months of labor, Quinn took the car north. En route to Oakland, Quinn and mechanic Claude French, learning that the race was cancelled due to rain, turned southward at Merced and headed for Los Angeles.

About five miles north of Fresno on December 13, 1931, Quinn's Model-A Ford roadster was sideswiped head-on by a northbound truck. The new Ford roadster was demolished and Quinn died on the roadside. The beautiful "Francis Quinn Special" Miller racing car he was towing was not damaged. French received only minor injuries. Manslaughter charges were filed against the truck driver, but later dropped by the forgiving Quinn family. Thus, Quinn, at 28, joined his close friend Walt May in death.

Never a drinker or smoker (he felt that alcohol would impair the steel nerves so essential on the track), Quinn was held in high esteem by thousands of fans who mourned his tragic death.

In his column, Sports Editor Sid Ziff of the Los Angeles Evening Herald and Express, said:

"It was the irony of fate, I suppose, which led Francis Quinn to be killed yesterday in an automobile accident on the public highway.

"For four years Quinn had piloted an automobile at dizzy speeds over perilous dirt race courses.

"He never so much has had a single accident.

"Strange as it now seems, he was safer at 90 or 100 miles an hour than he was on an ordinary automobile trip home.

"Automobile racers are fatalists. They see no reason why they should not take risks on the track. One and all believe that when it's time to cash in, they'll get it, no matter what they are doing.

"Oddly enough it worked out that way for young Quinn.

"Francis Quinn was one of the most popular drivers at Ascot. He counted everyone as his friend.

"In this way he was serious enough about his profession. He neither drank or smoked, because he believed it would impair the steel nerves so necessary in a grueling duel of speed."

Despite his nerve-shattering duels on the speedways, it was an incident only connected with racing that caused his death. Yet, it is ironic that Quinn had experienced only one minor accident on the speedway. That was in 1927 at Banning, when he spun out of control and struck the back straightaway fence. He received a gash on his forehead. After the injury healed the hair failed to grow back, leaving him partially bald. After he began winning races regularly, the press dubbed him the "Bald Eagle." His sobrique stuck with the fans. Fellow drivers kiddingly named him "skillet head."

For years Quinn was deprived of a chance to drive at Indianapolis because of a physical ailment. His heart was diagnosed as abnormally large. However, due to his Ascot success he got a chance to drive in the 1931 Indianapolis race. The AAA supported his pleas after he had won the 1930 Southwest title. (Fellow drivers also backed Quinn, saying that Quinn "had no heart" during his many Ascot speed tests). After qualifying his self-made "Tucker Tappet Special" hopped-up Model-T third fastest, behind Lou Meyer and Paul Bost, he was the first driver eliminated when his transmission broke on the third lap.

Quinn's body was returned to Los Angeles for funeral services and burial at Evergreen Cemetery. Affixed on his tomb is a miniature racing car in bronze. The inscription reads: "To Francis Quinn, Our Champion."

An ardent fan wrote a touching eulogy about Quinn, for his family and friends. It reads:

He goes in spirit 'round the track
Where once his courage mighty cheers awoke.
As of success his roaring motor spoke.
Success he would with calmest pleasure meet,
Defeat, with sportsman's smile, and clasp of hand,
Where once his name was swept from mouth to mouth,
Today his death is mourned throughout the land.
Then true to Francis Quinn his friends should be,
In honor of his mighty life so brave,
And bury not, there with his noble heart,
The love which should be his this side the grave.

(Courtesy, Molly Sinicrope, 1931.)

Left: Francis Quinn in his "Francis Quinn Special." He never got the "bugs" out of his $6,000 Miller Marine creation, the car he built during the 1931 season. One of Ascot's supreme heroes, he died on the highway following cancellation of a race at Oakland. **Bottom:** Quinn died beside the wreckage of his Model-A roadster. He was towing his Miller speedster when the accident occurred. **Lower left:** Quinn's tombstone at Evergreen Cemetery in East Los Angeles.

For the entire 1932 season at Ascot, the numeral 4 would be retired in remembrance of Quinn, who was fourth in Pacific Southwest standings at the time of his fatal accident.

For 1932, Bill White's new "Miller Special" that was assigned to Triplett, carried the numeral 1 on its tail and cowling for winning the 1931 title. Added coats of red lacquer paint, brightly nickel plated spoke wheels, exhause pipe, grill, oil pressure pump and brake handle, and a name change to "Red Lion Special," made the car the class of Ascot. With the resplendent Triplett seated in the cockpit, attired in red sweater and white cloth helmet (to match the car's colors) the combine was unmatched in capability and razor sharp appearance.

Triplett's chief competition in 1932 was Babe Stapp, Brunmier, Al Gordon, Sam Palmer, Kelly Petillo, Chet Gardner, Stubblefield, Spangler, Howdy Wilcox, Mel Kenealy, Bill Cummings, Wilbur Shaw, Cantlon and Bryan Saulspaugh. Saulspaugh was a newcomer from the midwest and billed as the "Midwest Cyclone." Also competing was ambitious Rex Mays.

Other flashy Miller powered racing cars came pouring into the famed track to seek gold and prestige. Stapp drove Chad McClurg's classy No. 15 "Gilmore Speedway Special," the first-ever 255 cubic inch Miller at Ascot; Brunmier switched from the Sparks No. 6 car to Harvey Ward's "Gilmore Speedway Special" No. 5; Stubblefield vacated the "Cragar Special" for the "Green Special" and the "Mallory Special," two speedplants from the midwest. Petillo and Cummings also drove "Lion Head Special" Millers. Spangler gunned the fast No. 19 "Gilmore Lion Special," and Kenealy throttled the good looking No. 18 "Earl Haskell Miller Spccial." Palmer, Gardner, Wilcox, Saulspaugh and Cantlon also ob-

tained speedy Miller racing cars.

Al Gordon, who debuted at Ascot in 1927 with limited success, was strictly a "Fronty" Ford driver in cars such as No. 56 "Dink Special" and the No. 61 "Prentiss Special." In 1932, Gordon got the No. 60 "Mahoney Special" Miller in which he began a steady climb towards racing success.

Earl B. Gilmore must be credited for his part in making Ascot a success. Gilmore, president of the Gilmore Oil Company, sponsored race cars at Ascot for many years. His "Gilmore Specials" with lion decals on their cowlings, gave the lineups a touch of class. Red and yellow colored racing cars were the standout of the era.

Crews and mechanics kept these cars polished and sharp to the delight of the fans. The hum of those Miller motors, the aroma of castor oil, and the glitter of plated racers, provided colorful racing fields.

Another highlight at Ascot was the introduction of the first crash helmet ever worn in competition on an American track. Crash helmets in the U.S. were unheard of at this time, and every driver used the old style cloth headpiece under his strapped goggles. Wilbur Shaw, who was to win three Indianapolis races, then received a gift that was to set the safety standard for all present and future drivers.

The gift was a crash helmet, given to Wilbur in the spring of 1932, by Major H.O.D. Seagrave, of England. Thus, Wee Wilbur became the first man to wear such a helmet on a U.S. track.

Shaw was resoundingly booed when he first wore the helmet. He was heckled by the speed thirsty fans and sometimes called "chicken." Many Ascot drivers refused to wear the helmet, for fear they would lose prestige and become targets of the howling fans. Then it happened:

Shaw was in a heat race one afternoon with Stapp, Sam Palmer, Saulspaugh and

Spangler. Shaw came out of the north turn too fast, smashed into the homestretch fence and flipped in his car towards the infield. Wilbur was ejected and airborne about 25 feet and landed on his head, shoulders and buttocks. He came out of the flight with nary a scratch! After the significant part Shaw's helmet played in preventing serious injury, or even death, crash helmets began to blossom at Ascot.

It was soon learned that book publisher, the late Floyd Clymer, had received a shipment of 40 crash helmets from England. Clymer perhaps anticipated their use would become mandatory, being of the same model Shaw wore in his accident, most of the drivers started wearing the heavy gear.

In March, 1932, "Midwest Cyclone" Bryan Saulspaugh got into Danny De Paulo's No. 22 "Gilmore Red Lion Special" and drove it sensationally. Actually, it was rotund Danny who unveiled the car at Ascot a few weeks earlier, in practice sessions. But Danny lost control one day and flew over the south turn fence. The shiny, new Miller was a total wreck and fast work was required to ready it for Saulspaugh and later, for Phil Pardee.

Not only did Saulspaugh breathe down Triplett's neck, he also won a couple of 100 lappers and elevated himself into serious title contention. But Ernie, sensing Bryan's possible "steal" of the title, responded with the "Red Lion Special" and won three main events in a row. The fans were more than convinced that Triplett was "it." Saulspaugh had his career cut short a couple of weeks later at Oakland. Slippery track conditions from a sudden light rain caused the wreck, it was reported. Bryan's two-seat Miller shot out of control and tore down the judge's stand. Officials at the starting line had scattered for cover and starter "Pop" Wagner was seriously in-

jured. Saulspaugh was killed instantly.

At this time Gordon had requested to drive Art Sparks' No. 6 Miller at Ascot, but was refused because Stubblefield's services were still demanded. Instead, Al drove the "Mahoney Special" to its limits. Mechanical wooes and other misfortunes plagued him, however, and Gordon would wind up out of the first ten for the 1932 season.

Suddenly, Les Spangler got into the hot competition. Les copped six straight "Helmet Dashes"—the fans shaking with enthusiasm over the kiss from various movie queens. The mustachoed throttle stomper had made a good comeback after his involvement in the three-car wreck of the year before, which claimed the life of George Young.

Colorful Wilbur Shaw also got into the fuss. Despite boos for wearing a crash helmet, Shaw stuck his foot into the "Mallory Special" and earned the crowd's respect by dogging Triplett all the way. Shaw, in winning a 100 lap main event, set an Ascot record of 46 minutes, 21 seconds, April 2, 1932.

A unique incident occurred one Wednesday night during the 75-lap main event. With Triplett on the inside of the front row, and Gardner on the outside, the field of 14 cars roared into the south turn as starter Bill Koller waved them away. Gardner, in his white No. 2 Miller. tried to grab the lead from his outside position by going high on the turn to get around Triplett. Chet, however, roared into the turn too hot and went into a broadslide. Meanwhile, Ernie, in the "Red Lion Special," hugged the inside of the track and Gardner's car smashed into the fence high on the banked turn. The machine wedged itself into the timber. Triplett whizzed by and led all the way to the checkered flag, while Gardner's car stayed stuck in the barrier and a disappointed Chet perched up on the fence and watched the entire race. In those days races weren't stopped unless wreckage was strewn in the path of racing cars. In this case Gardner's was completely out of the way, and officials saw no reason to halt the race and remove the car. (Such an official act would not be permitted today). How Chet got away with the idea of sitting on the fence to watch the race, is anybody's guess.

It was in 1932 when Bob Carey made his second appearance at Ascot. Carey, of Anderson, Indiana, appeared briefly the year before but had returned to more familiar midwest tracks. At this time, however, "Bullet Bob" was on his way to winning the AAA National title, due to his many wins on the circuit's mile tracks. Carey drove the "Francis Quinn Special" No. 8, but the car was not quite up to those of Triplett, Shaw, Cummings and the others. The Quinn car, still comparatively new, had those "bugs" that only more driving could correct.

One of the most unique finishes in the history of auto racing occurred at the American Legion Speedway on April 27, 1932. A capacity crowd was on hand and the fans were in a frenzy that Sunday afternoon. The incident involved Arvol Brunmier and a field of hotshots comprised of Cummings, Gordon, Triplett, Stapp, Petillo, George Conners, Stubby, Shaw, Palmer, Spangler and others. Arvol, the "Whittier Shiek," holder of the all-time night lap record of 26.92 seconds in the Harvey Ward No. 5 "Gilmore Speedway Special," had earned the pole position for the 100 lapper. Zoom. Arvol took a commanding lead and held on throughout the race—almost. Not even Triplett's "Red Lion" could catch him. Arvol was that hot. Brunmier set a dazzling pace and was on his way to sure victory. He had lapped the entire field, with one exception—Al Gordon,

Brunmier, on his last lap, roared down the back stretch and was about to pass Gordon to enter the final turn. Then it happened: Gordon's car hit an oil slick and spun as Brunmier approached him. Arvol's car couldn't miss the spinning Gordon and struck the car head-on. At impact, Arvol's speedster spun around and the motor began to sputter. The front-end was completely smashed in, the front axle bent, the front tires deflated and the front wheels pointed inwardly, like a pigeon-toed athlete. However, the motor didn't quit and it barely mustered enough power to push the car about five miles-per-hour—backward! Meanwhile, Babe Stapp had wrested second place from Triplett, and although a lap behind the front-running Brunmier, began to close ground at a rapid clip. Brunmier's motor finally quit and the car was coasting toward the finish line at five miles-per-hour, in reverse! Steering the car backward. Brunmier hung on while the on-rushing Stapp left the south turn and gunned his No. 15 Miller down the back stretch at terrific speed. Arvol was about 25 yards from the finish line. With only 10 yards to go Stapp shot out of the north turn. Zoom! But Brunmier's car barely limped across the finish line first, just as Stapp's car whizzed by at 115 miles-per-hour. Babe had missed victory by inches! Arvol received a standing ovation.

Another event, far different, was about to happen at Ascot. What created a lot of commotion and interest among the fans was Brunmier's wedding—on the track! The ceremony was held in view of the grandstand crowd and right in front of Harvey Ward's No. 5 Miller. The fans really got their kicks that night and showered Arvol and his bride with gifts. Fellow drivers, mechanics and officials did likewise as they surrounded the newlyweds. It so happened that Arvol's bride-to-be had agreed to say "I do" if the "Whittier Shiek" would quite racing. Bowing to her wishes Arvol and his fiance took their wedding vows. Bets had been exchanged among the drivers that Arvol wouldn't quit racing. After a couple of more races, however, he bade goodbye to Ascot, where he had gained the respect and admiration of the fans since 1926. There never was a night like that unusual wedding night—on a race track, many agreed.

Another driver bade adieu to Ascot, but in a different way. Fearless Nick Martino met his end in a unique accident off the track on August 9. Nick was exhibiting a "hop-up" before a group of enthused spectators on a vacant field at Third Street and Robertson Boulevard, Hollywood. During the "exhibition" the car flipped and Martino was crushed to death. Martino was considered a top prospect by Ascot fans.

No sooner had Brunmier and Martino departed from the Ascot racing scene than death struck with another sickening crash. On September 18, H. D. (Hal) Provan was involved in a fiery accident when his "Y Service Special" hopped-up Chevrolet hit the back straightaway fence while going into the north turn. The car skyrocketed some 25 feet into the air and burst into flames before 10,000 horrified fans. The inferno completely destroyed the racer.

Later in the 1932 season, Rex Mays abandoned his own "Mays Special" No. 71 and grabbed a ride in the aircraft engine powered "Hispano Special" which almost took wing. Rex, just a youngster, had his eye on Triplett, Gordon, Spangler, Cantlon, Shaw, Stubby and the rest of the Ascot demons. Although Rex couldn't quite keep astride with the hot Millers, his driving ability gave them all a rough time and an indication of what the future had in store for the top aces.

Gordon, in the "Mahoney Special," al-so had a bead on the winging Triplett, yet he too had trouble closing in on the "Blond Terror." Each Sunday afternoon and Wednesday night, it usually was Triplett blasting to victory, with Al, Stubby, "Wild Bill," Spangler, Shaw and Cantlon at his heels. Not far behind was ambitious Rex Mays.

One Sunday afternoon, Triplett held a comfortable lead, but out of nowhere came hot-footed Mays to wrest the lead from the impeccable Ernie and his refined "Red Lion Special." Rex floor-boarded the "Hispano" No. 21, but with five laps to go he hit somebody's oil, spun and smashed into the fence. Ernie regained the lead, screamed across the finish line a winner, and that was that.

Triplett was holding a comfortable lead late in the 1932 season. As he sped to his second straight title, not even the happy-go-lucky Al Gordon, Spangler and the other aces could match him, Triplett and the "Red Lion Special" combine was almost impossible to conquer, so decisively had he won the title.

The final standings for 1932 were 1—Triplett, 2—Spangler, 3—Shaw, 4—Chet Gardner, 5—Cummings, 6—Carey, 7—Babe Stapp, 8—Kelly Petillo, 9—Sam Palmer, 10—Brunmier, 11—Gordon, 12—Cantlon. Stubby was 15th that year. Mays placed 21st.

For 1933, Dr. Loring stuck with the Legion portion of the speedway's name, but changed the title to Legion Ascot Speedway from the previous American Legion Stadium. The new name appeared attractive and went over big with the fans. Thus LEGION ASCOT SPEEDWAY came into being.

Al Gordon finally got fired up and was able to match Triplett in ability and in racing equipment that year. Gordon obtained the No. 5 "Gilmore Special" which was built by crafty Art Sparks and capable Paul Weirick. The Sparks-Weirick bullet, a Persian blue, silver numeraled and nickel plated beauty really flew. The powerful Miller motor was of 220 cubic inches of displacement, and allowed up to 246 cubic inches. It was in this car that Gordon won the 1933 championship and set the Ascot lap record of 25.70 seconds.

The AAA Contest Board had initiated two "firsts" for the 1933 season—Class B point standings for drivers assigned to less expensive and inferior cars that were called "B" cars." That year the AAA was to provide championship points for both "A" and "B" cars. Drivers competing for the "B" title were such stalwarts as Ted Horn, Louie Tomei, Art Boyce, Swede Smith, Al Reinke, Woody Woodford, Bob Austin, Frenchie LaHorgue, Tommy Cosman, Tex Petersen, Pinky Richardson, A. J. Walker, Bob Gragg, Jimmy Miller, George Conners and others. The AAA also changed the racing title to Pacific Coast AAA championship. "Southwest" was deleted from the official racing title.

Triplett opened the 1933 season by winning the 100 lap feature on January 5. Gordon, however, began winning his share, and early into the season it was becoming noticeable who might be the new Pacific Coast champ. Gordon held a comfortable lead in point standings (not like Triplett's unsurmountable lead of the previous season) because of the rapid-fire and efficiency of the Sparks-Weirick speedster that was comparable to Ernie's "Red Lion Special" No. 1 in looks and in performance.

Another Ascot episode began to unfold at this time. After another brief absence, "Bullet Bob" Carey returned from the midwest. This time, though, Carey brought with him a big 255 cubic inch Miller racing car—the Joe Marks-owned No. 6 "Lion Head Special" out of Gary, Indiana. It was

March 2; the air was electric.

Carey first earned an "Ascot reputation" in 1931 (his first appearance) and **again** in 1932, when he finished sixth in Pacific Southwest standings. This time, however, Carey returned as National AAA champion for 1932, achieved for his many victories on the big-car circuit and for his stirring fourth place finish in the 1932 Indianapolis race.

After Gordon's sudden success in the Sparks-Weirick car, Triplett just as quickly regained his winning form by copping three main events in a row to press for point leadership. But Carey returned to Ascot just in time to snap Ernie's victory streak. Carey and Triplett, the fast qualifiers, were matched in the "Helmet Dash." Carey took the lead at the drop of the flag and he was never headed in the big Miller. The fans went wild as starlet Celeste Edwards planted a big kiss on Bob's chops. In the 100-lap feature event, Carey and Triplett battled for almost the entire race. Again "Bullet Bob" flashed to victory. The huge crowd roared its approval of the fearless, extremely heavy-footed but completely relaxed (behind the wheel) midwesterner.

Ascot was experiencing the fastest period in its history. The Millers were doing 120 miles-per-hour on the straightaways and averaging 90 miles-per-hour on the five-eighth's mile track. The 300 horsepower Millers took the track to their liking.

Carey had suddenly found himself in serious contention for Pacific Coast honors by matching Gordon and Triplett victory-for-victory. Gordon held the lap record (25.70 seconds) and Carey vowed he'd shatter the mark.

On April 16, 1933, during a Saturday afternoon practice session, Carey met with a fatal accident in the big Miller. Many heard him say how he'd break Gordon's record that day. Carey might have had he not encountered mechanical difficulty.

With several hundred "free" spectators on hand, Carey warmed the motor for a couple of laps and then got the big Miller going on the back stretch. At about 118 miles-per-hour "Bullet Bob" was entering the north turn . . . but he didn't make it. Instead, Carey plowed the big racer into the fence with a sickening blast. Likeable Bob never regained consciousness. He died of a broken neck.

It was surmised that the accelerator pedal became stuck, causing the car to enter the turn at top speed and strike the fence with full force. With Carey's life snuffed out, Gordon's lap record remained. Other drivers were to try, only to fail. Only Gordon himself would lower the record to 25.47 seconds on May 24, and set the all-time Ascot one-lap record.

Eddie Meyer, who had retired from Ascot competition, said he had begged the American Legion and the AAA to remove the iron railing they had installed around the north turn.

"I got in trouble with the officials for complaining . . . I didn't give a damn, though.

"Bob Carey would have gone through the wooden fence and shot right up the north turn hillside and possibly save his life. Instead he hit the new iron railing and was killed," said Meyer.

Meyer also said he asked the officials to dump mounds of dirt along the outside of the dangerous south turn and eliminate the perilous bank drop. "The cars would have leveled off instead of plunging down the bank. I got in trouble for that, too, so I gave up," he added.

The loss of National AAA champion Carey was mourned throughout the country and sobered thousands of Ascot fans. Carey always called Ascot "my favorite

track." Carey was a terror in the midwest circuit, as well, and his fearless duels with equally intrepid—the late Dutch Baumann —would never be forgotten.

The rivalry resumed between Gordon and Triplett for "King of Ascot" laurels and the race to the 1933 AAA Pacific Coast title took on heated proportions. The air was constantly suspensive. Each week it was Al and Ernie and young Rex Mays hooking up in wheel-to-wheel duels. Mays, in Paul Fromm's No. 21 "Hispano Special" started to show his prowess. Only Gordon's Sparks-Weirick Miller and Triplett's "Red Lion" could keep reckless Rex at bay. Rex then switched cars, vacating the "Hispano" for Eddie Winfield's more rapid, souped-up Model-B Ford "Winfield Special." Rex also drove the fast "Lion Head Special" Miller that year.

Things changed fast for heavy-footed Rex. Many times he'd come out of no-where and win his share of main events, heat races and "Helmet Dashes."

On May 21, one month and five days after Carey's fatal crash, Ascot had its second fatality of the season. Tom Forsythe, a newcomer, was battling front-running cars in a consolation race when his "Fronty" Ford clipped another car, spun out of control and smashed into the south turn fence. He was thrown clear but died instantly.

A little over a week later, May 30, 1933, Ascot veteran Spangler was killed in the Memorial Day race at Indianapolis. Spangler tried to overtake Malcolm Fox, shot out of control and crashed. Spangler and his riding mechanic, G. L. Jordan, never regained consciousness. Spangler had been a long-time Ascot favorite. He was to be sorely missed by Ascot faithful.

No sooner had Forsythe and Spangler been laid to rest that tragedy struck Ascot again—the year's third fatality at the dangerous track. On June 14, Frank Suess and

Frenchy LaHorgue tangled on the home straightaway during a five-lap heat race. Locking wheels, the cars flew over the fence just past the starting line and wound up beneath the lower portion of the grandstand. Suess, driving the "Stewar Special," was killed instantly. His car was a total wreck. LaHorgue was not injured, but the Frenchman never raced again. "This is it for me," LaHorgue muttered.

Another tragedy almost occurred on June 30. It happened during the 100-lap main event when Babe Stapp's car went out of control and threw him onto the track as speeding cars approached. The AAA's Art Pillsbury ran onto the track and pulled the stunned driver to safety. It was one of the most heroic acts ever seen on a race track.

For July 12, 1933, tire magnate Leonard Firestone became race referee, Reeves Dutton and Walter Shaw were technical inspectors, Edward Maly was secretary of the Technical Committee. Pit attendants were J. C. Winch and Vic Lindahl. Bill Koller became chief starter for the injured Fred Wagner. Assistant starters were James Grant and C. C. Ballenger, Ralph Hepburn was assistant scorer and Harrold Harper, assistant timer.

Departmentally, Henry Prussing was director of personnel, E. W. Gilliland was director of police. Neil McDonald replaced Norman J. Hartford as publicist. Fred Laing was director of parking, Carl Mathias was liaison officer. Legal adviser was James F. McBryde. Harry Schmidt remained as plant superintendent. Directors of the official program "Speedway" sale price, 15 cents) were "Reg" Regelin and Herb Marow.

Driver entries for the July 12 race were Triplett, Petillo, Gordon, Carl Ryder, Rex Mays, Mel Kenealy, Harry Jacquez, Charley Heisler, Tommy Newton, Stubblefield

and others. Newcomers to the speedway included Bob Gregg, A. J. Walker, Al Reinke, Jimmy Miller, Charley Oxenfeld, Roy Balaam and Bob Austin.

Triplett won the "Helmet Dash." Mays was second. Herb Balmer (an unexpected entry) won the first five-lap heat race, besting Swede Smith and George Conners. Art Boyce won the "B" heat race, heading Reinke and Louie Tomei. "Pinky" Richardson won the second "B" heat race, outgunning Bob Austin and Tommy Newton.

Triplett also won the 50-lap main event. Kenealy was second in the classy Earl Haskell No. 6 "Miller Special." Petillo, Ryder, Johnny Kreiger, Heisler and Jacquez trailed in that order. George Conners won the 15-lap "B" consolation race. Swede Smith was second, Jimmy Miller, third, and Al Reinke, fourth.

For the August 9, 1933, show, Harry Hartz replaced L. K. Firestone as referee. All other positions remained the same, for the Legion and AAA.

Mays won the "Dash" in 53.14 over Petillo and set the all-time two-lap record. Ted Horn beat Art Boyce in the three-lap "B" race. Swede Smith beat Horn, Reinke, Tomei and Babe Stanyer in the five-lap "B" race. Jimmy Miller won the next five-lap "B" race, out-dueling Frank Wearne, Richardson, Tommy Cosman and Charley Oxenfeld.

Mays showed Gordon the fastest way around the track by winning the 50-lap main event for "A" cars. Kenealy was third, followed by Herb Balmer and George Conners. Jimmy Miller wound up the evening by winning the 15-lap "B" consolation race, nosing out Louie Tomei and Babe Stanyer.

A capacity crowd was on hand the night of July 20, 1933, to see Gordon and Triplett hook up in the 75-lap main event. Triplett had won the "Helmet Dash" and a big kiss from starlet June Knight. (Miss

Knight had just completed the film, "Wake Up and Dream," which also starred the late crooner Russ Columbo). Gordon was on the pole in the Sparks-Weirick bullet for having the fastest qualifying time. Triplett was on the outside in his bright red "Red Lion Special" Miller.

The pair got off to a flying start, rounded the south turn and into the back stretch they flew, neck-and-neck, at more than 100 miles-per-hour. Ernie poured it on entering the north turn. But Gordon was also determined and kept the same speed. Triplett tried to pass Gordon on the outside but Gordon wasn't giving anything and stayed alongside. Suddenly, Triplett's car broadslided out of control, slid high on the turn, hit the fence and went over the barrier. The fans screamed as Triplett's car took a crazy hop and then rolled. Ernie was thrown from the car and knocked unconscious. Gordon slowed momentarily, steadied his car and breezed to the checkered flag.

Triplett was hospitalized for more than a month, but Ernie came back bravely and drove the repaired "Red Lion" at a dizzy pace. He couldn't, however, overtake Mays, who had grasped second place in the standings while Ernie had missed so many races.

Triplett was leading with 404.64 points when he was injured. Second was Mays (276.10). Next came Chet Gardner, Stapp, Kenealy, Cummings, Shaw, Petillo, 208.69; Gordon, 188.33. Following were Stubblefield, Ryder, Kreiger and down to Tommy Cosman with 15.32 points.

Swede Smith led the "B" car drivers with 188.27 points. Following were Ted Horn, George Conners, Louie Tomei, Al Reinke, Bob Austin and down to Babe Stanyer with 6.94 points.

Leading cars for cash award were Bill White's No. 1, Art Sparks' No. 5, Paul Fromm's No. 21, Earl Haskell's No. 18, Walt Harris' No. 2, and Kent Watson's No. 24. Leading "B" cars for cash award were Kay Tye's No. 45, Leo Monson's No. 32, Bill Rasor's No. 35, Joe Zottarelli's No. 36, Russ Garnant's No. 49 ,and Jack Duffy's No. 44.

On August 9, 1933, young and ambitious Tommy Newton was killed coming out of the south turn, making it four deaths in the season. The Long Beach youth tried too hard to pass a couple of cars, spun out of control and turned over with Tommy pinned underneath. The 15-lap consolation race was slowed while crewmen wiped oil off the track. Death was instant.

Ascot narrowly missed a fifth fatality on September 2. This time it was Harry Jacques who crashed while rounding the north turn in the "McDowell Special" No. 26. Jacques, a veteran driver, hit the fence at full force, went over the barrier and the car was a total wreck. The front axle and wheels were ripped off the chassis at impact. He cheated death miraculously.

The dreaded "Grim Reaper" was not through, however. The sixth death of 1933 occurred October 29. The victim: Babe Stanyer. A comparative newcomer, Stanyer met instant death when he bolted out of control entering the fatal south turn, went over the fence and rolled down the long embankment. Mortician Ivy Overholtzer was very busy that year, embalming Ascot's nervy race drivers.

By September 1, Gordon assumed command of the championship race. He won 80 per cent of the main events over the next three and one-half months. Gordon was the new champion, replacing Triplett. Swede Smith was crowned "Class B" champion. Ted Horn placed second, Conners, third, Tomei, fourth. Stanyer was at the tail end (in memorium) .

The death of veteran started Fred "Pop" Wagner was announced on November 13,

1933. Wagner succumbed due to injuries received in the April, 1932, racing accident at Oakland, in which driver Bryan Saulspaugh was also killed.

Following Gordon in point standings for 1933, were: Mays, Triplett, Petillo, Gardner, Kenealy, Herb Balmer, Carl Ryder, Wilbur Shaw, Babe Stapp, "Stubby" Stubblefield and Les Spangler (in memorium.)

Mascot Pictures in Hollywood rented the Legion Ascot oval, at the close of the 1933 season, for the filming of the auto racing melodrama—"High Gear." The 90-minute film starred James Murray as the racing "hero." His lovely leading lady and "bride-to be" was played by Joan Marsh. Youthful Jackie Searle was also top cast. As usual, Ascot drivers provided the "reel" action.

Spot anyone you know or knew? It's 1932 at Legion Ascot Speedway, where time out was taken for a bit of photography at finishing line. No. 2 car at left, already warmed with canvas over the radiator, is Chet Gardner's "Miller Special." Kneeling from left are Les Spangler, Al Gordon, Chet Gardner and Carl Ryder. Standing, from left, are Art Pillsbury, Dale Drake, Eddie Offut, Ed Wintergust

Sam Palmer, Wilbur Shaw, (with crash helmet), blank, Russ Garnant, Danny DePaulo, blank, blank, blank, Red Garnant, George Connor, Mel Kenealy, Tommy, Newton, blank, Harvey Ward, Babe Stapp, Ernie Triplett (partial head), Kelly Petillo, blank, blank, Mel McKee, blank, blank. Can anyone fill in the blanks?

The one and only Ernie Triplett, 1931-32 Pacific Coast AAA champion. Bill White's "Red Lion Special" and intrepid Ernie made a great pair in 1933. It was this evening, however, when Triplett and Al Gordon tangled on the north turn; Ernie wound up with a month's hospital confinement.

Ernie Triplett in Bill White's famous Miller. Ernie's the champ and that's the late Dale Drake of Offenhauser racing fame, far right. Drake and Louie Meyer later produced the Meyer-Drake Offenhauser engine, son of the famous Miller. At center is Ed Wintergust, a Richfield Oil Company representative.

A pensive Ernie Triplett contemplates strategy for start of a main event. Note rope tied to front axle and frame used to pull cars for start. Men from left are Ed Wintergust, Eddie Offutt and Dale Drake, extreme right; owner Bill White's car crew. AAA official Art Pillsbury wears checkered cap. (Doug Boyd Collection)

Eighteen-year-old motion picture star Joan Blondell presents Victory Crown Helmet to Ernie Triplett after "Helmet Dash" win in 1932. Miss Blondell appeared also as advanced publicity for the current motion picture "The Crowd Roars," which was filmed the year before at Ascot. The car is the No. 6 Allen Special.

(Doug Boyd collection.)

The glory was all Ernie Triplett's this 1933 evening when he won the "Helmet Dash" in a heated battle with Al Gordon. That's Bill White's "Red Lion Special." The gal is actress June Knight, who made a stopover at Ascot while filming "Wake Up And Dream" which also starred famed crooner Russ Columbo. Triplett, however, was injured in that night's main event, when he tangled with Gordon on the north turn. Al was only slightly injured, but for Triplett it was a month's hospital stay.

Ernie Triplett poses proudly with his daughter Doreen. It is March 20, 1933, Ernie is the Coast champ. Food donations went to the poor that day. Triplett was born in 1907 at Paris, Illinois.

Ernie Triplett wins "Helmet Dash" in the "Allen Special." Ernie was flying high during the 1931 Pacific Southwest championship. Who's the gal?

A truly great driver was "Blond Terror" Ernie Triplett, 1931-32 Pacific Coast AAA champ. The car is Bill White's "Red Lion Special."

Some guys have all the luck," Ernie Triplett might have thought s Kelly Petillo whizes by in the Sparks-Weirick Miller speedster. riplett blew a tire on the "Red Lion Special" and managed to iss the fence during an August 9, 1933, race.

Ernie Triplett took a rear view pose in Bill White's "Red Lion Special" in 1932. Ernie was set to qualify. Yes, he nabbed the pole, won the "Dash" and main event.

It's October 29, 1933, main event, with Al Gordon leading as the cars enter the north turn coming out of the back stretch. Rex Mays in the "Hispano Special" No. 21 is second, followed by Floyd Roberts in third spot and Ernie Triplett, fourth. Gordon won it, but was hard pressed by the rookie Mays. (Art Sparks collection.)

Happy-go-lucky Al Gordon in the Sparks-Weirick "Gilmore Special," 1934. Gordon won the 1933 title in this car and also set the all-time Ascot lap record of 25:47 seconds. Al died on Ascot's south turn in 1936. One of the track's all-time greats.

Al Gordon pulls into Ascot pits after qualifying for the day's racing card. The 1933 Coast champ is in the Art Sparks-Paul Weirick "Gilmore Special" Miller.

Al Gordon offers victory smile after winning 150-lap main event in 1934. Gordon's car, the Sparks-Weirick Miller Special," carried a numeral 1 for winning the 1933 title. Art Sparks, left, mechanic Sid Swaney, right. (Art Sparks collection.)

It was Al Gordon's turn to win the "Helmet Dash." But who is the lady? Oldtimers, please step forward and identify her.

Al Gordon guns Art Sparks' powerful Miller into the lead on the opening lap of an October 5, 1933, main event. Ernie Triplett is in second place followed by youthful Rex Mays in the "Hispano Special" No. 21. Gordon won 100 lapper on way to the 1933 championship. (Art Sparks collection.)

Ernie Triplett and crew, 1933. Two straight Coast titles is deserving of such a picture. That's Dale Drake, extreme left, with Eddie Offutt at Ernie's left. Ed Wintergust, Richfield Oil Company representative, is at right. The car is Bill White's "Red Lion Special," natch.

Herb Balmer, after a Wednesday night Ascot heat race.

Ready for action is Al Gordon, 1933 Pacific Coast AAA champion. Gordon looks determined in the Sparks-Weirick "Gilmore Special."

"Crash helmets are here to stay . . . let's hope," Rex Mays and Ernie Triplett say. The pair reflect on Bryan Saulspaugh's flip of Danny De Paolo's Miller, in superimposed picture. Actually, the helmet saved the life of Triplett, seated in Bill White's "Red Lion Special," in which he was seriously injured a week later in a duel with Al Gordon. The pair display the different style of helmets, ruled mandatory for all drivers in 1934.

Screen star Claire Windsor presents Rex Mays the Victory Crown after rapid Rex won the two-lap "Italian Helmet Dash" on November 6, 1933.

Youthful and handsome Rex Mays, who provided thousands of thrills for as many fans during a colorful racing career which began at Colton Speedway, continued spectacularly at Ascot and on other tracks of the country.

Rex Mays, another victory . . . another smile. This time it was a 75-lap main event at Ascot. The year is early 1934.

Rex Mays married his school-days sweetheart, Miss Dorothy Grunwald of Riverside in 1933. Rex celebrated with a 100-lap main event win.

Rex Mays, 1934-35 Pacific Coast AAA champion. Seated in Paul Fromm's "Winfield Special" hopped-up Model-B Ford. Pictured at Ascot, 1934.

Bill Hart learned that sometimes a racing car can "bite" gnawingly as evidenced by this October 28, 1933, wreck over the south turn fence. Miraculously, Hart emerged unscathed.

Red Clark flipped over the north turn fence and was killed in this 1934 accident. His "McDowell Special" received a battering at impact . . . indicative of the force by which he struck the wooden fence and plowed into the field outside the track.

Harry Jacques was another torrid leadfoot at Ascot. Jacques met his end in a street accident in 1938. It's a Wednesday night at Ascot.

Daring Wilbur Shaw allowed his big Miller to get away from him which flipped against the south turn fence in this May 10, 1933, wreck.

After striking the south turn barrier Rex Mays' car went into a roll in a cloud of dust and overturned. The intrepid Riverside driver miraculously escaped serious injury.

Three of the most prominent racing drivers who appeared at Ascot during the track's heyday, are, from left: Al Gordon, Ernie Triplett and Rex Mays. Gordon, killed at Ascot in 1936, was Coast champ in 1933. Triplett, who lost his life at El Centro in 1934, was Coast champ in 1931-32. Mays won Coast honors in 1934-35 and was fatally injured at Del Mar, California, in 1949.

(Art Sparks collection.)

One night, Carl Ryder spilled oil all over the Ascot track from his leaking car, yet the nervy driver "stuck it out" for a few more laps before being black-flagged by the officials. Ryder, depicted on April 13, 1931, was suspended for a few races but came back strong to continue hounding his racing buddies.

Art Boyce, long-time Ascot favorite, turned to auto racing after a stint as an ambulance driver. In fact, Art returned to his former trade after he quit racing.

Chris Vest, a capable driver who drove against Ascot's best since 1929. Chris's only problem was getting a good car to drive regularly. Yet, he always gave the top notchers a run for it.

"Stubby Stubblefiled began driving "class" cars in 1932. Here he's set to fly in Art Sparks' "Miller Special." "Stubby" wasn't the first to drive the new Miller; Arvol Brunmier made its debut six months earlier.

The "Stewar Special" car which was driven by Frank Suess, Stan Hallet, Frank Wearne and other Ascot drivers during the 1933-34 seasons. Owner of the car was Stephen Newmark.

Earl Mansell gets ready for 1932 main event in a double overhead cam Fronty which was built by Roscoe Ford. Norm Thompson and Alvin Kingsley are from left to right. Man on right unidentified. Earl years later became mayor of Chula Vista, California.

"It was a pleasure," says Al Theisen after winning a heat rac[e] in 1934.

"This is some car," mused Kelly Petillo, after he had qualified fastest and thus earned the pole position in the "Helmet Dash" and main event. Kelly's time was 26 seconds flat in Art Spark's terrific Miller. It's 1934 and Kelly, the 1935 Indianapolis 500 winner, is happy.

"Bullet Bob's" big Miller powerplant. Bob Carey, 1932 National AAA champion, on his last day of life. It is April 16, 1933, just minutes before his fatal smashup on the north turn. Carey was out to break Al Gordon's one-lap record. A stuck accelerator pedal and collision with a newly-installed steel railing ended his life. The car is Joe Marks' "Lion Head Special" of Gary, Indiana, a 270 cubic inch job.

Babe Stapp hailed from San Antonio, Texas, but he found a "second home" at Ascot. A driver in Ascot's first race in 1924, Stapp drove many racing cars and wound up in 1933 with Chad McClurg's 255 cubic inch "Gilmore Speedway Special." This was the first 255 ever driven at Ascot. Babe drove in 13 races at Indianapolis Speedway, too!

An unidentified women sits in Chet Gardner's No. 2 Miller. That's Chet right behind her (with helmet on). Kelly Petillo stands at left. He's also wearing a helmet.

Frank Suess lies draped outside his disabled "S & S Special" after it threw a wheel on the north turn at Ascot, 1932. Suess miraculously escaped serious injury. However, he was killed the following year in a two-car wreck on the main straightaway.

(Courtesy Roscoe Turner.)

Drivers come and go, but none were more ambitious than Tommy Newton. He was tough on Culver City and San Diego tracks and was billed a "comer" at Ascot. But the fatal south turn proved Tommy's undoing in 1933. Standing at center is driver Red Clark. Joe Zotterelli, left, was mechanic on the "Champion Special."

Youthful Tommy Newton was killed at Ascot in 1933 when he lost control going into the south turn on the 13th lap. The San Diegan drifted up to the fence and was thrown out of his car.

Tommy Newton was a young and aspiring driver until his untimely death in 1933 at Ascot. Newton is seated in the car in which he was fatally injured on the south turn.

Tommy Newton met death in the "Quinn Special" on the south turn on August 9, 1933.

Tommy Newton's fatal wreck at Ascot on August 9, 1933. Al Reinke zooms by in the "Duffield Special."

Arvol Brunmier and his bride-to-be Clara Smith at the Los Angeles Courthouse steps, after they had made application for a license to marry in 1932. They were married right on the Ascot main straightaway. This car is a Bugatti.

"Yes dear, I'll quit." That was Arvol Brunmier's promise to his bride, the former Clara Smith, before taking their vows on Ascot's home straightaway in 1932. The race car is Harvey Ward's "Gilmore Speedway Special." Brunmier set the night lap record of 25:92 seconds the week before. For the record, Arvol didn't keep his promise, made a brief comeback, then quite Ascot competition forever.

Blur of lights and crowded grandstand indicate "night action" in 1933. A fair view of the south turn and main straightaway. Wednesday night racing was popular with the fans.

Arthur Langlo, Wednesday night heat race entrant at Ascot Speedway, 1933.

Art Sparks' "Poison Lil" car powered by a Miller engine, had four Linker carburetors. "We ran only three races and set three track records; at El Centro, Ascot and Oakland. Art Pillsbury ruled them off and allowed only two carburetors," said Sparks. The name "Poison Lil" derived from a spoof on Ernie Triplett and his wife Lillian, for Ernie's unsuccessful bid to beat out Al Gordon for the Coast 1933 title. Here's Gordon after he won another "Helmet Dash." Is the gal actress Toby Wing?   (Art Sparks collection.)

Mel McKee, a native Kansan who thrilled many a folk at Ascot during his hay-day in racing. Mel often times, with a heavy foot emplanted on the throttle, won his share of the prize money. This is Mel on June 30, 1930.

Ray Pixley (depicted on August 9, 1935), who hailed from Fullerton, California, was a standout driver at Ascot until the track's demise in 1936. Pixley was fatally injured at Roby, Illinois, after a series of tries in the Indianapolis 500.

Earl Brentlinger was among a group of racing drivers and mechanics involved in the controversy evolving from the funeral in 1934 of famous driver Ernie Triplett. Brentlinger is depicted as a driver on October 17, 1932, at Ascot.

Little Buster Gourley feels the head dress of a race driver. Ascot ace Arvol Brunmier ties the helmet on the youngster.

Bill Cummings seated in Art Sparks' rapid Miller. "Wild Bill was a colorful sight as he drove with his shirt sleeves rolled upward and shirt-tail blowing in the breeze.

Mel Kenealy's crewmen prepare the "Haskell Miller Special" for a practice stint at Ascot. Careful inspection was a necessity. Owner Earl Haskell is at left.

Mel Kenealy, 1929 Pacific Southwest champ is pushed off by crewmen for a Saturday afternoon warmup on June 22, 1933. The car is Earl Haskell's classy "Miller Special."

Long preparation came to an abrupt halt for Mel Kenealy during a Saturday afternoon practice sprint on June 22, 1933. Mel threw a wheel while steaming into the south turn on the first lap in the Earl Haskell "Miller Special."

From left are Ted Horn, Al Reinke, Babe Stapp, Earl Brentlinger and Jack Savage, who were brought to District Attorney Buron Fitts' office for identification. An inquiry was held to determine the identity of the men who slugged a news cameraman and kidnapped a reporter at the funeral of ace driver Ernie Triplett in March 1934. Fitts banned racing in the Southland until his office had learned the identity of the alleged assailants.

It was a series of controversies that rocked the Ascot confines from the result of Ernie Triplett's death at El Centro, California. Listening to an ultimatum by Dist. Atty. Buron Fitts are drivers, from left: Al Reinke, Babe Stapp, Earl Brentlinger and Tony Gulotta and the AAA's Art Pillsbury. Fitts ordered no more racing in the county until "all kidnapers of James Lee and John Bennus, newspaper reporter and photographer, are turned over to the district attorney's office." Seated is attorney H.L. Pratt.

Louie Meyer, left, and Rex Mays inspect Rex's motor in the Hispano No. 21 mount. Mays was hotter than blazes during the 1933 season. Meyer, on July 20, said Mays was a coming champion . . . the greatest prospect he had seen in years. He was so right.

Lester Spangler made it a habit of winning the "Helmet Dash." Fact is, Les copped six in a row. He's proud of becoming once again the bearer of the Victory Crown helmet. It's 1932, a year before the fatal smashup at Indianapolis.

For Lester Spangler, it was a hair-raising battle for the 1932 Pacific Coast AAA title. Aggressive Les, however, had to settle for second place behind the intrepid Ernie Triplett. Les is seated in the Walt Harris "Gilmore Red Lion Special" Miller on April 2, 1933, just one month before his fatal accident at Indianapolis Speedway.

Les Spangler gets ready to qualify Danny DePaolo's No. 19 "Gilmore Lion Special." Spangler ranked high among the contenders for the 1932 title when this picture was taken. Les was killed the following year at the Indianapolis Motor Speedway.

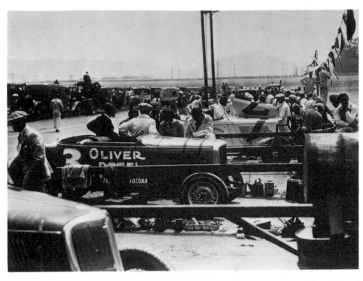

Ascot pits during preparations for Targo Florio, 1934. Chet Gardner (hatless) stands by his car No. 7. Red Clark, second from right, stands by his No. 3. (Courtesy Roscoe Turner.)

Preparing for the 1934 Targo Florio road race at Ascot is veteran driver Eddie Meyer. Eddie, who had entered the Mines Field road race when this picture was taken, drove this car in the Ascot race.

Targo Florio action, 1934. Sam Palmer, car No. 28, leads Mel Kenealy, car No. 18, and Rex Mays, car 21. Louie Meyer won the long grind, over the hills and around the track. Ted Horn placed second. More than 25,000 fans attended.

"Stubby" Stubblefield practicing for the 1934 Targo Florio. It's a 1934 V-8. Outside car and giving "Stubby" direction downhill is earlier day racing pioneer Eddie Pullen. (Courtesy Roscoe Turner.)

Another view of 1934 stock cars in Targo Florio action. Louie Tomei leads Red Clark and Eddie Meyer. Al Reinke was killed while practicing for his race. Beside the grandstands, trees and hillsides, many fans scaled freight cars lined along Valley Boulevard to watch the race won by Louis Meyer.

(Courtesy Roscoe Turner.)

"The Midwest Cyclone." That was Bryan Saulspaugh's monicker during his hey day at Legion Ascot Speedway. Picture taken inside pits in 1932. Car is Danny De Paulo's "Gilmore Lion Special."

Bob Carey, 1932 National AAA champion (No. 6), goes into spin as Al Gordon weaves by, calmly and steadily. Action in north turn, a few weeks before Carey was killed in the "Lion Head Special."

Bryan Saulspaugh was a real ledfoot from Indiana. The "Midwest Cycline" is in Danny De Paulo's Miller mount in 1932. He was killed the following year at Oakland. Standing alongside is actor Jason Robards. That's Art Pillsbury in background with cap on.

Bob Carey loved winning the "Helmet Dash" at his favorite race track—Ascot. Winning the Dash sharpened him for a heat race and main event. He receives the Victory Crown helmet while seated in Francis Quinn's No. 8 Miller.

One of the closest finishes in auto racing history. Arvol Brunmier is congratulated and swarmed by admirers after his thrilling finish when he edged Babe Stapp by a few inches on April 27, 1932. Arvol coasted across finish line backwards after his car had collided with Al Gordon's mount, causing damage to his car. Stapp had unlapped himself and just barely missed beating Brunmier to the finish line. Brunmier had set the night record of 25:92 second earlier in the evening.   (Courtesy Arvol Brunmier.)

Record breaker Arvol Brunmier behind wheel of Harvey Ward's Miller mount. He's being congratulated by Reg Regelin, left, public address announcer, and track superintendent Harry Schmidt. In this car, Brunmier set the all-time Ascot night lap record of 25:92 seconds, in 1932.   (Courtesy of the late Arvol Brunmier.)

Mel Kenealy, 1929 Southwest champ, ordered a soft drink while displaying Earl Haskell's classy No. 18 "Miller Special" in Hollywood. The year is 1933.

White shirted Bill Cummings was recipient of the Victory Crown helmet for a "Helmet Dash" win. The Sparks-Weirick "Gilmore Special" bullet was to his liking on this 1933 day. Bill won at Indianapolis the following year.

Bill Cummings in the "Sparks-Weirick Miller Special" leads Ernie Triplett through north turn on January 1, 1933. Triplett drives Bill White's "Red Lion Special."   (Art Sparks collection.)

Hey! You're going the wrong way! "Wild Bill" Cummings put too much on the throttle and went into a spin at Ascot, 1932. Bill's in the Art Sparks-Paul Weirick "Gilmore Special."

Action down the Ascot homestretch in 1932. Mel Kenealy leads Ernie Triplett. In third place is Sam Palmer, with Chet Gardner, Kelly Petillo and Wilbur Shaw (sixth in the "Mallory Special") following in that order.   (Doug Boyd collection.)

Mel Kenealy had vacated the "Haskell Miller Special" in 1933 for a ride—and victory— in the "Helmet Dash" in the "Neves Special." Actress Loretta Young? does the honors of presenting the 1929 Pacific Southwest champion the Victory Crown helmet.

Ascot Speedway, 1924-1936. The 5/8'ths mile track where many great drivers risked life and limb in achieving high speed glory.

Arvol Brunmier leading the way during a 1932 five-lap heat race. Arvol's in Harvey Ward's speedy Miller. At his tailpipe is "Stubby" Stubblefield. Behind "Stubby" is Ernie Triplett. Wilbur Shaw is next, followed by Kelly Petillo. Yes, Arvol won it.

Lineup of drivers and mechanics at Legion Ascot Speedway in 1933. Standing, from left: Rex Mays, blank, Babe Stanyer, George Conners, blank, Ted Horn, Clyde Adams, blank, Swede Smith (peering from rear), Earl Brentlinger, blank, Wilbur Shaw (wearing crash helmet), Babe Stapp, Al Gordon, blank, Woody Woodford, blank, blank, Louie Schneiter, Chet Gardner, blank, blank, Al Reinke, Tommy Newton, Kelly Petillo. Kneeling, from left: blank, blank, Danny Oaks?, Tommy Cosman, Harris Insinger, blank, blank, Art Boyce Sam Palmer, Shorty Cantlon, Bill Cummings, Mel Kenealy, blank, Art Sparks, Bob Carey, Ernie Triplett, "Stubby" Stubblefield, blank, Tony Radetich?, blank. Will someone please come forward and fill in the blanks and correct us where necessary.

(Art Sparks collection.)

The famed Gardner brothers, Ray, left, and younger Chet. They were the first brother pair to drive on a major race track.

Chet Gardner slams into the fence as Ernie Triplett goes by. Gardner tried to take the lead at the start from the front row, outside position. Car stayed wedged in fence while Triplett went on to win at Legion Ascot Speedway, 1932.

"Anybody for a challenge?" Rex Mays is at the Ascot starting line in Paul Fromm's "Winfield Lion Head Special" in 1934. Rex was Coast champ that year. He repeated in 1935, too!

George Conners dented up the "Gilmore Lion Head Special" on October 29, 1933. George received only bruises.

Bill Koller waves his flag to signify victory for Arvol Brunmier in Harvey Ward's car. Ernie Triplett finished second with Bob Carey third in this 1932 "Helmet Dash."

CHAPTER V

END OF AN ERA

(1933 - 1936)

❧

Gordon Battles Mays

Death Toll Rises

Press Slams Ascot

Ernie Triplett "Retires"

El Centro Tragedy

Controversial Headlines

Another Targo Florio

Mays Snatches Crown

Two-Man Indy Cars

Gordon-Matlock Crushed

Grandstand Burns

A Final Death

Farewell to Ascot

Legion Ascot Speedway reached its peak in popularity from 1928 through 1934. However, many unfortunate incidents were to force the track's closure by 1936, much to the dismay of the faithful fans who had supported the spectacular speedway since its inception in 1924.

Ascot had begun to succeed financially in 1928, when American Legion Post 127, Glendale, California, took over the promotions. From that time on, attendance climbed steadily. Net revenues from 1928 to 1931 ranged from $15,000 to $40,000 per season. The peak financial years were enjoyed during the 1932-33 seasons, with a net intake of $50,000 and $60,000, respectively. Considering the depression years, revenues gained were considered excellent.

What attributed to Ascot's financial boom was the influx of rapid and classy "Miller Special" racing cars, cash awards for pit crews and cars. Free admission for practice sessions, 100-lap and 150-lap main event attractions, colorful "Helmet Dash" presentations, attendance by movie stars, the fierce competition between great drivers, all of which can be credited to the Legion and the American Automobile Association's Western Regional Office.

But the spectre of the "Grim Reaper" continued to show its ugly face, and that alone led to the track's disappearance from the racing scene. Six deaths in 1933 did little to ease the frustrations of the AAA and the American Legion. The end of Ascot was nearing.

Despite the fatalities, 1933 had been a thrilling year for fans to remember. Al Gordon won most of the main events, "Helmet Dashes" and heat races to replace the great Ernie Triplett as Pacific Coast champion. Besides setting the all-time one-lap record of 25.47 seconds that year in the No. 5 Sparks-Weirick "Gilmore Special," the Persian blue, nickel-plated bullet would carry a silver numeral 1 during the 1934 racing season, emblematic of winning the 1933 Pacific Coast title.

Gordon himself had been involved in many spectacular wrecks at Ascot, on other West Coast tracks, at Indianapolis and on eastern tracks. Somehow he always managed to escape without serious injury. For that lucky streak he was nicknamed "happy-go-lucky Al." Gordon was well liked and the Long Beach ledfoot (by way of Redlands) always gave the fans their money's worth. He was sensational while dethroning Triplett as champion in 1933.

A story appeared in the newspapers which caused mixed emotions among the fans and drivers. Triplett announced his retirement. Many fans were disappointed because they would miss him. Whether his competitors were elated for no longer having to breathe his exhaust fumes, cannot be said . . . but might be assumed. Regardless, Triplett chose to retire from a sport he had dominated for so long. It was surmised that Ernie chose only to quit smaller track racing and concentrate on his life-long dream—to win the Indianapolis 500 miler.

At the close of the 1933 season, Astor Pictures rented Ascot for the filming of "Roaring Roads," an action-packed auto racing melodrama and Ascot's top drivers provided the action. Produced by William Berke, the film's "racing star" was an undistinguished actor named David Sharpe. His leading lady was pretty blond Gertrude Messinger. Also in the picture was veteran actor Jack Mulhall, star of the chapter play "Burn 'em Up Barnes" which was filmed at the track earlier that year.

Racing cars spotlighted in "Roaring Roads" were the "Atlas Chrome Special" and the "McDowell Special." Seen in live action were the No. 2 "Elwyn Holt Special" driven by Floyd Roberts and Bill Cummings in the No. 6 "Sparks-Weirick Special." There were several accident scenes, including Tommy Newton's fatal crash, and the wreck in which Mel McKee was thrown from his car but suffered only a broken leg.

During the last two months of 1933, however, Ascot had been beset by some adverse publicity.

Newspapers, seeking to capitalize on the spectacular wrecks and fatal accidents (to sell newspapers), "went to war on the joint," as it was voiced by the Ascot publicity staff. Some of the headlines read:

"She Sees Mate Fight for Life in Flaming Car."

"AAA Chiefs Will Make Racing Safer."

"Auto Racing Faces Storm of Protests."
"See Death for a Dollar."

"Many Join War Against Auto Racing."

The controversial publicity (mainly by the Hearst Corporation papers) got so heavy and thick, track superintendent Harry Schmidt announced his retirement. "Too much bad publicity," Schmidt stated.

The 1934 season then got off to a flying start, with champion Al Gordon taking a slight lead in championship points during the first three months. Young, fast improving Rex Mays was right on Al's tail in the ultra-fast No. 2 "Winfield Special" Model-B.

On March 13, 1934, the AAA scheduled a 100 lap race on the El Centro, California, mile dirt track. This race was to have much influence on the closing of Ascot.

The El Centro race should never have been held. The track was in poor condition on race day due to inactivity. Recent rains had caused a quagmire, then came a dry spell which hardened the surface. A quick watering down did little good. However, due to commitments the race was permitted to go on.

Triplett announced he would make a comeback by entering the El Centro race. This alone helped boost attendance and much interest. Triplett would compete against Gordon, Mays, Kenealy, Swede Smith, Harris Insinger and others who were gunning to win the Coast title. Many fans were still questioning Triplett's comeback plans.

Despite being away from competition for three months Triplett qualified fifth fastest in the Bill White "Red Lion Special" now carrying numeral 3 for its third place finish in 1933. Gordon had the front, pole position.

At the drop of the starting flag, Gordon took the lead in the No. 1 "Gilmore Special" and held a slight edge for seven laps. It didn't take long for clouds of dust to swarm over the track and made it difficult to see. In swirling dust, Swede Smith tried to miss Jimmy Wilkinson's stalled car on the center of the north turn, but his vision was blocked. Boom! Smith's car plowed into the stalled racer and he was thrown onto the track in view of the grandstand crowd. Smith lay motionless. Mechanic Hap Hafferly ran from the pits and gallantly tried to pull the stunned driver out of the path of speeding cars. Triplett, coming on like blazes . . . his car screaming through the dust storm . . . swerved wildly to miss the pair but struck Hafferly. Ernie's powerful car then vaulted out of control and smashed into Gordon's car. Triplett and Gordon flipped wildly, Gordon's car coming to rest on its wheels, Triplett's machine smashing against the fence and turning over. Hafferly was killed instantly, Triplett was on the track and dying. Smith, the 1933 "Class B" champion, died a few hours later. Gordon miraculously escaped serious injury, walking away with only a bruised arm. The race was stopped immediately and not resumed . . .

frightening repercussions were heard throughout the grandstand.

With the death of 27 year-old Triplett, Smith, 35, and Hafferly, 31, the adverse publicity steamrolled. The deaths created a sensation in the papers. Pictures of spectacular wrecks could be seen constantly spread over the front pages.

Triplett's funeral was attended by hundreds of fans. Babe Stapp, Mays, Louie Meyer and Earl Brentlinger were pallbearers. Ted Horn was heard to whisper, "Ernie never should have tried a comeback . . . this jinxed him . . . he should'nt have tried it."

The funeral was also the scene of some unusual happenings. A newspaper photographer had been dispatched to take pictures of the rites. Irate over the picture taking and fearing more adverse publicity for the racing fraternity, a group of drivers and mechanics roughed up the photog, took his camera and shuffled him away in a car. The photographer (James Bennis) was forceably taken to his newspaper office, where the men admitted the kidnapping but also demanded retractions for any pending bad publicity.

Triplett's death and the kidnapping of the photographer created an even bigger sensation. The bombardment, particularly in the Hearst papers, reached a new high. More headlines read:

"Assemblymen Join War Against Auto Racing."

"Auto Racing, Brutal, Says Barney Oldfield."

"Widow-In-Waiting-Faints-As-Mate's Car-Goes-Into-Spin."

"Just To Provide a Thrill."

"Is The Price Worth It?"

The headlines and stories were accompanied by pictures of Triplett's spectacular wreck and those involving the deaths of Bob Carey, Babe Stanyer, Herman Schurch, Tommy Newton, Red Clark, Earl Farmer, Kenny Morgan, Dud Ludwig, Kenny Stoddard, Bud Snavely, Lynn Eldridge, George Young, Frank Suess, H.D. (Hal) Provan and Tom Forsythe.

More sensational headlines were to follow due to the kidnapping and beating of the photog. Some read:

"Seven Racers Answer Edict."

"Fitts Issues Ultimatum to Drivers." (District Attorney Buron Fitts had been brought into the controversy) .

"Stop Auto Racing."

"Fitts Hurls Threats of Raid on Ascot Track."

"Racers Face Kidnap Charges."

Meanwhile, the AAA had scheduled a Targo Florio race at Ascot for April 15. The huge promotion, which would draw 25,000 fans, had been planned months before. The American Legion elected to resume Ascot promotions despite the wave of controversial publicity. Therefore, Post 127 would help the AAA in the Targo Florio promotion.

"The fatalities didn't make the Legion want to withdraw from promotions," said Dr. Loring, head of the Legion's Contest Board. Dr. Loring, asked about the Hearst newspaper war against Ascot, said:

"He (Hearst) was a sensationalist. I don't feel that he really wanted to close the track. I never thought of him that way. He was strictly a sensationalist . . . that's how he built his empire. We didn't like the bad publicity, but most of us felt no animosity towards him."

However, track superintendent Schmidt had a different opinion. He said years later:

"The wrecks and deaths had nothing to do with the bad publicity. It just happened that GM (General Motors) got sore at the Ford Motor Company, because the Fords were winning most of the stock car races in those days.

"General Motors told the newspapers it would pull out its automotive ads if Ascot held the Targo Florio stock car race. Ascot went ahead and held the race anyway. The ads were cancelled. Hearst and the other papers wanted the GM advertising, so Hearst decided to wage war against Ascot for running the race."

Edwin C. Austin, track business manager, had an opinion of his own. Said Austin:

"We were doing great up to the time (1933) when Mr. Hearst ruined the track's activities with his adverse publicity. Hearst blamed Ascot for other fatalities on other tracks . . . I mean to say Hearst used other fatals to reflect on Ascot deaths and accidents. Hearst killed it" (Ascot).

Austin added, "We (the Legion) were highly successful, financially. We gave plenty of money to charity . . . to Boy Scouts and to other group activity. The track under the Legion was constantly successful."

It was Austin who headed the Food Committee that would arrange food donations (to the poor) as the admission price to the races. The food donation drive paid off handsomely for the needy, as thousands of canned goods were collected at the track.

Seven drivers and mechanics were given fines and short jail sentences due to the kidnapping incident. Among the drivers were Louie Tomei and Indianapolis veteran Tony Gulotta.

For the Targo Florio, Pacific Coast and National circuit drivers were signed to compete. Stock cars, mostly Ford V8's, were used. Chevrolets, Willys. Plymouths and DeSotos were also entered. Like the 1926 Targo Florio, the 1934 race was scheduled for 200 miles on a 2½ mile course over nearby hills and around the track in the opposite direction. Extra grandstands in the infield were added, swelling the seat capacity to 25,000. The course was laid out by the AAA's Art Pillsbury and Robert Rowley of the Race Board of Control.

Three days before the race, with all drivers warming their cars in practice, driver Al Reinke was fatally injured while practicing on the hilly, tricky course. Reinke was testing a car owned by Louie Meyer. The car slid out of control and turned over. Strangely, Reinke's death received very little notice in the papers.

The day before Reinke's death another Targo Florio entry was also killed, but not on the track. Herb Balmer died in a street stock car he was driving near York Boulevard in the Los Angeles suburb of Eagle Rock. Balmer's death, as did Reinke's, received little publicity.

Warmups continued. Among the drivers were Louie Meyer, Danny DePaolo, Louie Tomei, Babe Stapp, Chris Vest, Red Clark, Chet Gardner, George Conners, Al Gordon, Kelly Petillo, Jimmy Wilkinson, Fred Frame, "Stubby" Stubblefield, Cliff Bergere, Jimmy Miller, Mel Kenealy, Rex Mays Sam Palmer, Ted Horn and Pinky Richardson. After a day's postponement due to rain, the race was held.

With an estimated 25,000 fans on hand (several hundred more climbed nearby freight cars to watch), Louie Meyer driving a Ford V8, found the hilly course to his liking and held the lead for several laps and coasted to victory. Horn was second. Then came Gordon, Begere, DePaulo, Stubblefield, Mays, Woody Woodford, Chet Gardner, Eddie Meyer (Louie's brother), and down to last place Richardson.

Richardson's Willys drew cheers because of the little car's difficulty in surmounting the hill behind the regular track's back stretch, and for its ability to glide like a bird on the way down. Pinky got rousing cheers for his efforts and for finishing the race.

Meyer and Horn waged a bitter battle. At one time it was believed that Ted would "take" Louie when Meyer's car went into a skid, but the old master soon had control and posted his big win.

After the Targo Florio the track was again rented by the movie makers. This time "Born to Speed" starring Richard Arlen, was filmed. Actual speed duels between Mays and Petillo in flashy Miller cars, provided the action. Handsome "Daredevil Dick" played the hero's role.

When the big cars returned for an April 24 show, in order to slow down the big Millers, the AAA reduced the engine displacement for non-supercharged cars to 200 cubic inches from a previous 220 cubic inches.

Mays was turning laps almost as fast as Gordon in the No. 2 "Winfield Special." Gordon, in the Spark-Weirick "Gilmore Special" had all he could handle to stay even with Riverside's pride and joy. Mays soon started taking the play away and speeding towards the 1934 Pacific Coast AAA title. Curious officials would sometimes inspect Mays' motor, but found nothing illegal.

Not only was Mays a great driver but a very popular one. Rex was particularly popular with youngsters, whom he enjoyed having around his racing car after winning a main event. Mays and the red and yellow "Winfield Special" presented quite a picturesque sight.

Mays was out-dueling the veteran Gordon and leaving the fans gasping in wonderment over his heavy foot. Not even Petillo in the Harvey Ward Miller, the veteran Mel McKee, Floyd Roberts in the No. 5 "Worley Special" and Harris Insinger in Russ Garnant's No. 12 "Miller Special" could stay with him. "Stubby" Stubblefield

tooled the Earl Haskell Miller, but he had difficulty with "Rexless Rex." Mays was absolutely spectacular in pursuit of the championship.

But on August 8, 1934, youthful Ed Haddad qualified in 26.58 seconds, got the pole position and beat Mays in the "Helmet Dash." From then on the 22-year-old throttle stomper from Inglewood commanded respect from the other drivers.

Two weeks later it was movie making time again at Ascot. Nat Levine's Mascot Pictures began production of a twelve chapter play "Burn 'em Up Barnes," starring Jack Mulhall, Frankie Darro and Lola Lane for the Saturday matinee crowd. Racing scenes were filmed by Mays, Gordon, Petillo and other speed merchants. The serial went over big and the fans could see their favorite track on the movie screen, each Saturday for 12 weeks.

On August 4, the promoters staged a 100-mile motorcycle race over a road course, outside and on the inside of the track. The winner was Ray Eddy of San Francisco. Second was Buck Lishman. Byrd McKinney was third. Recalled is the fans' howling for the race cars to return to action and dump the two-wheelers.

Dr. Loring announced his retirement as chairman of the Contest Board, effective October 1. He was replaced by Henry Prussing. All other Legion and AAA personnel remained the same.

Driver entries for the November 12 card were Gordon, Mays, Petillo, Gardner, easterner George "Doc" McKenzie, Floyd Roberts, Red Clark, Ray Gardner, Hal Cole, Bob Sall, Bob Austin, Bruce Denslow, Harris Insinger, Clyde Bloomgren, George Conners Jimmy Wilkinson, Frank McGurk, Lane Curry, Pinky Richardson, Johnny McDowell, Stan Hallett, Louie Webb Al Putnam, Ray Durling, Ted Horn, Ralph Gregg Bob Gragg, Ray Pixley, Frank Wearne and Harry Lester.

Mays led the point getters with 460.98. Roberts (422.35), Petillo (200.93), Gordon, Conners, Clark, Wearne, Pierre Bertrand, Cole and down to Louie Webb, with 11.63 points.

Leading car owners for cash awards were Russ Garnant, Paul Fromm, Leo Monson, Paul Weirick, Henry Puckett and Al Morales.

Best appearing cars were Henry Puckett's No. 57, driven by Ted Horn; Jack Duffy's No. 34, driven by Lane Curry; Ed Winfield's No. 2, driven by Rex Mays; Walt Harris' No. 18, Ray Gardner's No. 12; Earl Haskell's No. 4, driven by Kelly Petillo; Chet Gardner's No. 5; Bill White's No. 1, driven by Al Gordon; and Henry Stephens' No. 6 Miller, driven by George Conners.

Best Appearing Car and Crew point leaders were Wearne, Norman Muir, Wilkinson, Bruce Denslow, Chet Gardner, Mays, Petillo, Johnny McDowell, Horn, Conners, Cole, Gordon, Ray Gardner.

The November 12 card featured a long 250-lap main event. Although Mays held a good lead in point standings, he had not yet cinched the title. Mays and Roberts had been engaged in heated warfare and chunky Floyd still had a chance. But on this day, Gordon took command and beat them both.

After Triplett's death, the wrecked Bill White-owned "Red Lion Special" had been rebuilt. When the car returned to Ascot it had been re-painted a beautiful white with blue numeral 1 and blue flame design. It was loaded with nickel plating. It also carried a name change of "Bill Froelich Special" for its new sponsor, who operated a Los Angeles Ford agency.

With Gordon behind the wheel, the rebuilt Miller set a sizzling pace during the entire 250 laps and won before more than 12,000 fans. Gordon received a standing ovation. Petillo had taken over the Sparks-Weirick Miller car after Gordon signed to drive White's rebuilt speedster for the extra long race.

Mays was able to fend off challenges by Roberts, Petillo, Gordon and Insinger, to capture the 1934 title. The final point totals read: Mays, 478.73; Roberts, 425.37; Gordon, 321.53; Petillo, 214.6; Insinger, 179.36; Conners, 156.42; and on down to George Robson with .93 points.

With the big 250 lapper in his hip pocket to close the 1934 season, Gordon hoped that being assigned to Triplett's ill-fated car would lead to another championship in 1935. Mays, however, had other ideas.

Since Gordon had vacated the Sparks Weirick bullet, Mays also made a switch. Rex vacated the "Winfield Special" Model-B and signed to drive the Sparks-Weirick car in which Gordon set the Ascot lap record.

The Sparks-Weirick "Gilmore Special" was still a rapid piece of machinery as all 1935 drivers were to find out. The car also was re-painted—a bright red and yellow. The only mechanical change was the installation of a red-hot supercharger which made the Miller whine with power. Everybody, even those outside the track, knew when Rex was on the track winding 'er up. Adverse publicity had somewhat cooled and Mays anxiously awaited the 1935 season for the chance to equal Triplett's successive Pacific Coast titles.

Racing opened at a boiling pace in January. Roberts had a new car—the flashy looking No. 2 "Elwyn Holt Special" Miller. Gordon stayed with the rebuilt Bill White car. Insinger remained behind the wheel of Russ Garnant's No. 12 "Miller Special." Petillo drove Earl Haskell's No. 4 "Lion Head Special" and George Conners was in the No. 7 Miller. Ted Horn tooled the No. 10 "Atlas Chrome Special." Chet Gardner piloted the No. 17 "Miller Special."

Young and ambitious drivers continued to fill the program. There were Hal Cole, Frank Wearne, Roy Russing, Pierre Bertrand, Lane Curry, Johnny McDowell and Bruce Denslow. Others were Ed Haddad, Frank McGurk, Onyx "Bud" Snavely, Bob Austin, Ray Pixley, Tex Peterson, Rajo Jack (Jack DeSoto, one of the few Negro drivers), Danny Oakes, Jimmy Miller, Mel Hansen, George and Hal Robson, Freddie Agabashian, Duke Dinsmore, Earl Mansell, Fred Winnai, among others. But Mays and the Sparks-Weirick Miller were too much to overcome. Rex remained hot for the entire season . . . he wasn't headed en route to his second straight Coast title. Solid equipment abounded at Ascot, but Rex and the whining supercharged bullet that Art Sparks and Paul Weirick cared for so delicately, led all for the 1935 crown.

Each Sunday afternoon's hot 100-lapper featured Mays, Petillo, Roberts, Gordon and Insinger fighting for the lead. They were the class of Ascot. Racing pictures appeared daily in newspapers. One edition depicted the No. 4 Petillo car in the lead, and the Mays No. 1 car in close second. The caption read: "The Beginning of the End." A bottom picture also showed the front-running Rex on way to winning, with Kelly second. Another photo erroneously identified Gordon as trailing Wilbur Shaw. Actually, it was Bill Cummings, not Gordon. Faithful fans asked for a correction, and the same picture appeared the following day with the heading: "Wild Bill is Right." Obviously the fans were very much interested in accuracy.

Insinger pulled a fast one on the "big four" (Gordon, Mays, Petillo, Roberts) on March 1. Mays and Roberts were in front with the handsome Harris in fifth spot when Gordon and Mays spun to avoid Tomei. Big Roberts and Petillo also spun

to avoid a crash. Insinger didn't slow down a bit, instead weaved through the whole pack, didn't touch a thing and blazed to a 100-lap victory. Mays had won the dash the week before and a kiss from starlet Rene Whitney, but this day belonged to Insinger. Not only did he win the main event, he had won the "Helmet Dash" as well and a big smooch from equally lovely, the Swedish woman racing driver Greta Mollander.

The "death bell" had not rung at Ascot since Reinke's wreck in the Targo Florio practice of almost a year before. On March 31, 1935, however, the "Grim Reaper" returned. Onyx "Bud" Snavely crashed to his death while qualifying. Snavely's car shot out of control in the south turn and went over the fence. Like many before, the car rolled down the bank.

The popular Insinger was fatally injured soon after his "big day" at Ascot. It happened April 14 on a 100 miler at Oakland. Insinger and Gordon were dueling vigorously when they became tangled. Insinger plunged over the fence to instant death. Again Gordon escaped unscathed.

In May, Ascot lost another of its old-time favorites. "Stubby" Stubblefield was killed while qualifying for the Indianapolis 500 miler. Gold-toothed Stubby, a regular Ascot contestant since 1926, was sorely missed by the fans and racing world. Kelly Petillo, driving a "Red Lion Gilmore Special," won the big Indy event that year.

Another historical incident occurred June 21, 1935—the announcement that the Legion would bow from Ascot promotions. Henry Prussing advised that Post 127 no longer would be connected with future Ascot racing. What was to be the next-to-last race under Legion promotion, developed into a very hot duel between current champion Rex Mays and ex-champ Al Gordon. Although Rex had the fastest qualifying time, 26.44 seconds to Gordon's 26.49 seconds time, Gordon out-drove Mays in the "Helmet Dash" and repeated in the 100-lap main event.

In the dash, the pair went into the first turn, hub-to-hub. Gordon didn't yield a thing, and when Mays let up on the accelerator Al poured it on, grabbed the lead and won the two-lapper in a scorching 54.85 seconds. Al received a starlet's kiss and a batch of flowers from Legion officials for his victory.

One week before the Legion bow-out, Loren "Red" Clark was killed at Ascot. Perhaps Clark's shattering wreck more than convinced the Legion that it was time to end its promotions.

The Legion's final show was on June 21, 1935. As if to bow out in a blaze of glory, the Sunday afternoon show was a thriller. Mays beat Gordon in the first heat, Conners took the second heat. Tomei won the third five-lapper. Harry Lester copped the 15-lap consolation race.

Mays had a comfortable lead on way to his second straight Coast AAA title, but Gordon, gunning to regain lost prestige, was determined to win that 100-lap main event. At the wave of the starting flag from Bill Koller, Rex and Al screamed into the south turn neck-and-neck. Al was in Bill White's Miller, Mays in the Sparks-Weirick bullet. As Mays let up Gordon again poured it on. Al held the lead throughout the 100 laps. Mays challenged all the way, the rapid Miller being no less than a half-car length behind. Roberts was third, Pixley, in the "Morales Special" No. 86, fourth Following were Conners, Chris Vest, Hadded, Frank McGurk, Bertrand and Ora Bean.

With the Legion out of the Ascot picture, Bill White took over the track's promotions under a new banner: ASCOT MOTOR SPEEDWAY. (White was owner of Al Gordon's car). To keep the press off his back White cut a safer half-mile course inside the larger 5/8th mile. Mays won the majority of races, but the smaller oval didn't appeal to the fans. Attendance sagged and fans began howling for action on the bigger track.

Hoping to boost attendance another special show was held: midgets versus big cars in a series of match races. Mays and Gordon drove their larger Millers. Bob Swanson, Karl Young and Curley Mills wheeled outboard midgets. The midgets beat the bigger cars because they could drive the turns wide open on the smaller half-mile track, while the big Millers had to slow considerably. A capacity crowd watched curiously, but enthusiastically.

White then conceived the idea of featuring Indianapolis two-man cars for Sunday, December 15, 1935. The plan—big Indy two seaters for a 200-lap grind proved to be a sensational promotion. The country's best drivers were entered. As an added feature, fans got in free by donating a can of food for the poor. (The donation program date had been arranged by the Legion months before its bow-out). Kids under 12 were admitted free.

Promoter White signed up the best drivers. Drivers and their riding mechanics were: Rex Mays and Takio Harishima, No. 33 "Gilmore Special;" Al Gordon and Spider Matlock, No. 6 "Cocktail Hour Cigarette Special;" Floyd Roberts and Romeo Parenti, No. 22 "Golden Mash Special;" "Wild Bill" Cummings and Harry Dean, "Miller Special" No. 1 (Cummings was National AAA champion); Chet Gardner and Bob Biggs, No. 10 "Miller Special;" William "Shorty" Cantlon and Bert Lustig, No. 14 "Nick Lutze Special;" Wilbur Shaw and Eddie Demaree, No. 9 "Lion Head Special;" Lou Moore and Lyman Spaulding, No. 7 "Burd High Speed Special;"

166

Fred Frame and Val Pender, No. 23 "Catfish Special;" Louie Meyer and Eddie Meyer, No. 36 ''Ringfree Special;" Mauri Rose, in the No. 16 twin stacker; Louis Webb, in the Gilmore "Cat Fish" racer No. 15; and Babe Stapp and Aud McPherson, No. 66 "Scully Special."

The promotion drew 35,000 spectators. The infield also was filled as were nearby hills and trees along the south turn. Although it was one of California's all-time auto race attractions, the race never should have been held. First, the cars were too big and powerful for Ascot's five-eighth's track. Secondly, they would prove to be the downfall of Ascot . . . disaster would strike at a later date.

Mays grabbed the lead on the 125th lap and snared the 200-lap race and a big jackpot. Louie Meyer and his riding mechanic-brother, Eddie, finished second. Gordon, despite mechanical difficulties (he needed repairs which cost him 15 minutes), put on a burst of speed to finish third, Shorty Cantlon, Frame and Louie Webb were fourth, fifth and sixth.

For January 5, 1936, Ascot officials were listed accordingly: Capt. Eddie Rickenbacker, chairman of the Contest Board; Art Pillsbury, AAA regional director; Bill White, chief Steward; Frank Elliott, referee; Norman Hartford and Matt Gallagher, publicists; Joe Helget, personnel director; Ken MacKenzie, assistant personnel director; Ken Barton, KMPC radio announcing; Van Newkirk, public address announcer; Gilmore Oil Company, gasoline service; Southern California Plating Company, tow service; Charles Reising, concessionaire; Bill Koller, starter; George Stephenson, chairman of the Technical Committee; Bill Claus, pit manager and technical inspector; Reeves Dutton, technical inspector; Edward Male; secretary of the Technical Committee; Vic Lindahl, pit

attendant; Walter L. Smith, auditor.

On January 5, 1936, the regular single seat racing cars returned. It was to be their last appearance. Under White's promotion, Roberts, Ray Pixley and some two dozen other drivers competed. (White had relented to the crowd's plea to bring back the single seaters on the bigger five-eighth's track).

Roberts won the final race in the No. 2 "Elwyn-Holt Special." It was a 100-lap scorcher. Pixley in the "Morales Brothers Special," finished second. Horn, Denslow, McGurk, Bill Lipscomb, Duke Dinsmore, Bayliss Leverett and Louis Tomei finished in that order.

Because the first 200-lap race featuring Indianapolis two-man cars was a huge success, White came right back with a similar promotion on Sunday, January 25, 1936. Again a crowd of more than 35,000 attended. It was to result in tragedy . . . and the downfall of Ascot. The same drivers and their riding mechanics were spotlighted.

Gordon and his big No. 6 "Cocktail Hour Cigarette Special," with mechanic Matlock seated alongside, took the lead and held it for several laps. It appeared that Gordon and Matlock were on their way to sure victory. Mays, Meyer, Roberts, Cummings and Gardner chased him. Gordon steadily opened up a wide lead, Al appearing to drive the big 270 cubic inch Miller like a single seater. Gordon's car, which also was owned by White, was painted white and blue identical to the smaller single seater three-quarter car.

On the 117th lap Gordon lost the lead when his car broke a wheel. He immediately came to the pits for repairs. With a new wheel mounted, Gordon set sail after Mays, who had taken the lead.

On the 127th lap, Gordon blazed into the south turn too hot. Midway through the turn he skidded some 250 feet and struck the fence with thundering force, then rolled crazily down the embankment. Gordon and Matlock were crushed under the racer and received their final checkered flag. The stands became silent. Would Gordon walk away from that wreck as he had so many times before? It wasn't to be.

Mays went on to win his second 200-lap victory for the big cars. Meyer again was second, followed by Roberts, Cummings and Gardner. All other cars failed to finish. It really didn't matter because promoter White, soon after, quietly padlocked the track. White perhaps was convinced that to promote another race would have touched off a wave of indignation from the press and politicians. Thus, Ascot was closed—forever.

It was years later when Eddie Meyer, who had ridden as mechanic with brother Louie, told of the danger that existed outside the south turn where Gordon and Matlock and so many others crashed. "It seems that a contractor who had nothing to do with the track, was allowed to store a lot of heavy grading equipment just outside the turn. Al and Spider just plowed into that heavy machinery . . . they had no chance," he related.

About eight months later the entire grandstand was swept to the ground by a huge fire. The big structure burned quickly. Some say that several tramps who slept regularly underneath the wooden tiers, set the blaze to avenge for the loss of their favorite drivers down through the years.

The last bit of action at Ascot was staged in 1937. With the big grandstand's ruins and rubble removed, a smaller, temporary grandstand was erected for the filming of a final motion picture. Midget driver Bob Swanson is remembered screaming down the home straightaway in a big Miller racing car while the actors went into action and the cameras ground away. The movie's title is long forgotten. That, too, doesn't really matter, because Ascot closed its doors forever, right after that picture was filmed.

A year later, however, the track produced still another fatality, perhaps to end its history on the disastrous note—Ascot style.

Some youngsters, in a nervy effort to play racing driver, took to the track in a hopped-up roadster. One youth, who was riding in the rumble seat, was ejected as its driver lost control and flipped. The lad died instantly. The city then took quick action. With big bulldozers, workmen dug several ditches across the track to prevent more tomfoolery and avert another disaster.

What passed on was one of the most spectacular and colorful tracks in the history of automobile racing.

It is true that "Speed, Victory and Death" was Ascot's forte.

It is also true that Ascot was king of the roaring road.

You could say, "Auto racing can go on for another thousand years, but never, NEVER will there be another ASCOT SPEEDWAY."

You know, you might be right.

THE END

Pierre Bertrand in his "Bertrand Special" in 1934. Famed mechanic Clay Smith, right.

Pierre Bertrand flips his "Bertrand Special" on Ascot's back stretch. George Conners zips by. Bertrand escaped with minor injuries.
(Courtesy Roscoe Turner.)

Rex Mays and his riding mechanic Takio Harishima were the winning pair during Ascot's final two races featuring Indianapolis-type two-man cars. The pair won the first 200-lapper in December, 1935, and made it two straight with a victory in January, 1936. The Miller powered car was built by Art Sparks and competed at Indianapolis.

(Art Sparks collection.)

Lineup of some of the drivers and mechanics before the start of Ascot's last race in 1936. Kneeling at far right is Romeo Parenti. Standing, from left, are Rex Mays, Fred Winnai, Lou Moore, Chet Gardner, Bill Cummings, Fred Frame, Al Gordon, Eddie Meyer, Wilbur Shaw, Cliff Bergere, Shorty Cantlon, Doc McKenzie, Floyd Roberts and Takio Harishima.

Indy two seat cars enter the north turn during Ascot's final race on January 25, 1936. Floyd Roberts and Romeo Parenti lead Bill Cummings and Harry Dean. Third in the "Catfish" are Fred Frame and Val Pender. Fourth is Chet Gardner and mechanic Bob Biggs.

Rex Mays holds steady lead over Chet Gardner as the pair battled in Ascot's final race on January 25, 1936. The Indy two-man cars, although rather large for the 5/8ths mile track, put on a good show for the 35,000 attending.

(Art Sparks collection.)

Riding pals to the end were Al Gordon and "Spider" Matlock. This most intrepid pair is seated in the "Floating Power Special" at Mines Field (now International Airport) in 1934. They lost their lives in Ascot's final race on Jan. 25, 1936.

The final race . . . the final racing deaths. Al Gordon and "Spider" Matlock ripped out several hundred feet of guardrail before plunging to their deaths on January 25, 1936. It's the last checkered flag for a pair who had cheated death many times . . . for many years.

Youngsters being admitted into the Ascot track. Their admission price was canned goods for the poor. The day: December 15 1935. The event: the first of two Indy type two-man car races. Legion officials assist in stockpiling the donations.

Starter Bill Koller waves checkered flag to Rex Mays during "Helmet Dash" win. Breathing Rex's exhaust fumes is Kelly Petillo.
(Cortesy Roscoe Turner.)

Rex Mays and riding mechanic Takio Harishima, after winning the first of two two-man car races at Ascot on December 15, 1935. Rex was very popular with the fans. As usual, the heavy-footed immortal is surrounded by a crowd of admirers.

Rex Mays and Takio Harishima, in Art Sparks' No. 33 "Gilmore Special," prepare to pass Louie Meyer and Eddie Meyer (car No. 36) on way to victory in Ascot's last race. In third place is Floyd Roberts and mechanic Romeo Parenti. Meyer drove the "Ringfree Special," Roberts tooled the "Golden Mash Special." Movie camermen take precarious stand outside south turn fence.
(Courtesy Roscoe Turner.)

"Bearded wonder" George "Doc" McKenzie, who hailed from Eddigton, Pennsylvania, was a terror on many dirt tracks. He was featured in Ascot's two final races of Indy cars. "Doc" was killed in a 100-miler at Milwaukee.

Can food day at Ascot! Kids by the hundreds . . . perhaps thousands, were admitted free into the races. Cans of food as price of admission went to the needy. What a bargain to watch the best drivers in the best cars on a most famous track.

ft to right are Al Gordon, Floyd Roberts and Rex Mays. In jest, e trio makes adjustment on Gordon's "Cocktail Hour Cigarette ecial" twin seat Miller powered racer that was driven at Indian- olis and in Ascot's final two races.　　(Art Sparks collection.)

Frank McGurk continued racing long after Ascot closed in 1936 and became chief mechanic for several Indy cars. McGurk was regular "Class B" entrant at Ascot between 1933 and 1935.

E. C. "Woody" Woodford came to Ascot early as 1929. Woody looks determined in the "Duffield Special" in 1933. Pit crewmen are the Famalero brothers. The car was sponsored by Johnny Duff. Ed Winfield built this speedster.

Al Gordon in his "hot car," the "Bill Froelich Special." It's 1935; Al had lost his Pacific Coast AAA title to Rex Mays. The car is the former "Red Lion Special" in which Ernie Triplett was killed in 1934. Bill White owned the car, but auto dealer Froelich sponsored it.

Swede Smith, of Portland, Oregon, was making great strides in auto racing until his death at the El Centro mile dirt track in 1934. Smith was involved in the smashup which also killed Ernie Triplett and mechanic Hap Hafferly. Swede was 1933 Class B champ and was ranked high among Class A drivers in 1934. This car is the "Vieux Special" owned by Lloyd Vieux.

Veteran driver Babe Stapp presented a smiling Rex Mays with the Victory Crown helmet for winning the "Helmet Dash" in 1935. That's the re-painted Sparks-Weirick "Gilmore Special" in which Al Gordon set the all-time Ascot lap record two years previous. Mays was Pacific Coast AAA champ that year; he won in 1934, too, but in Ed Winfield's car.

Bruce Denslow, 1934, ranking Class B driver. Denslow was a "comer" but departed Ascot action after the final regular racing program in 1935.

Louie Tomei, in 1934. It's the "Zottarelli Special" with owner Joe Zottarelli alongside. Tomei, a very competent driver, became a movie stuntman in Hollywood. He died from the result of a studio mishap in 1956.

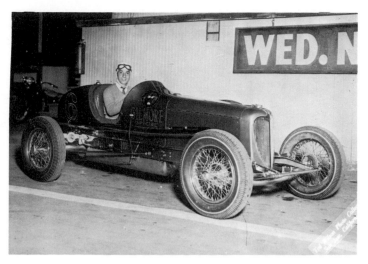

Kelly Petillo (1935 Indy winner), "Gilmore Special." Legion Ascot Speedway, 1933.

Is this Johnny Stricker's car? By the way, who's the driver? Any old Ascot fans around who can answer the question?

Danny Oaks was one of many young drivers to invade Ascot as early as 1931. Danny for years had his ups and downs until he landed the "Courtesy Corner Special" for the 1935 season. Oaks later became a very prominent midget driver.

Floyd Roberts in the "Elwyn Holt Special," a Miller. The year: 1935. Big Floyd was second to Rex Mays for 1934 Pacific Coast honors. Notice car's hooks hanging from front axle. This was a "safety" feature; in the event a wheel was thrown, the front axle would not dig itself into the pavement and throw the car out of control.

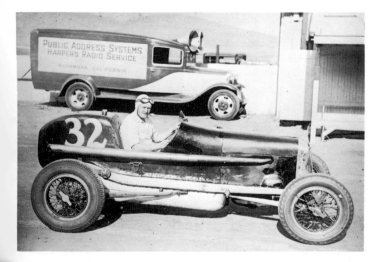

Norman Muir was another late arrival at Ascot. Norm was a "Class B" competitor when this picture was taken in the "R and R Special" in 1934. That's Harrold Harper's p.a. truck in background. Harper, who introduced the first electric timing system at Ascot, provided his services at the famed track for several years.

Bob Sall was Eastern dirt track champion and came to Ascot to drive this car for Ray McDowell. Modest Ted Horn said he never could, despite being National champion three years in succession, drive as well as Sall. Opinions are left up to old-time racing fans' conjecture.

Willie Utzman explains the Winfield flathead to driver Ed Haddad. The car had the famous Model-B Ford engine that led several main events and bested even the DOs and Millers, but would "blow" due to tremendous RPMs (8-9,000!).

(Doug Boyd collection.)

Ed Haddad brought a heavy foot to Ascot and drove impressively until the track's demise. Car owner Willie Utzman vowed not to shave off his beard until Haddad won his first race. In 1934, Haddad won a "Helmet Dash" and Utzman emerged clean shaven for Ed's next race. Mariorie Rambeau presents Ed the Victory Crown after his stirring "Dash" win over Harris Insinger, who drove Russ Garnant's rapid No. 12 Miller.

Harris Insinger, a top-notch driver who gave Ascot speedsters plenty of headaches. Insinger drove his last race at the famous Oakland Mile in 1935.

Philadelphian Harris Insinger was a very popular driver at Legion Ascot. Likeable Harris is at the starting line . . . on the pole . . . for the "Helmet Dash." He won that day in Russ Garnant's "Miller Special." It's 1935 . . . death would claim him a few months later at Oakland. (Any empty seats?) The car is the same machine which Ernie Triplett drove to Pacific Coast titles, 1931-32. The car was based on the remains of the Miller 91 that Frank Lockhart drove at Indy in 1926. Bill White bought the car from Alden Sampson. White sold this car to Russ Garnant, whose driver was Carl Ryder in 1934. It had bright red paint job with silver numeral 12 when Insinger drove it in 1935.

Ted Horn in the "R and R Special," 1934. Horn competed at Ascot, on and off until 1934, and went east to compete in Midwestern and Eastern circuits. Ted eventually was three-time National big car champion. He was killed at Duquoin, Illinois, in 1948. (Courtesy Roscoe Turner.)

Ted Horn's last ride. It's 1948 at Du Quoin, Illinois. The three-time National champ is placed on a stretcher after his accident on the second lap of a 100-miler. The Ascot veteran died a few moments later. Twenty years before, he began racing at Ascot.

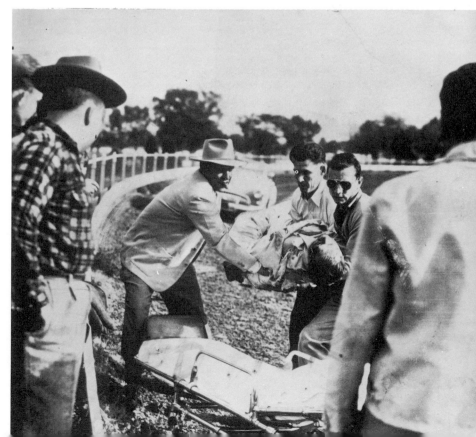

Ted Horn was a youngster at Ascot in 1928, who one day would be National big-car champ in 1946-47-48. In 1928, Ted sustained severe injuries which laid him up for three years. He returned to Ascot; despite limited success at Ascot, made racing history in Midwest and Eastern circuits.

Floyd Roberts was "hot stuff" at Ascot in 1934. The car is Russ Garnant's rapid Miller. Floyd won Ascot's last regular main event of 100 laps for single seat cars on January 5, 1935. Roberts won the 1938 Indianapolis race and died there in the 1939 race. Floyd hailed from Van Nuys, California, and believe it or not, raced in Ascot's first race in 1924.

Ray Pixley, in a 1935 Ascot pose. Ray drove for the Morales brothers that year, but had his fatal crash at Roby, Illinois, in 1936. Pixley was one of Ascot's top drivers until his final race.

George Conners was one of Ascot's better drivers in 1934-35. He drove this Miller at a pretty rapid clip. George drove many years at Indianapolis after Ascot closed. He also was a midwest and National competitor and gave the boys many a tussle.

Seven's a crowd. Rex Mays, first row on outside. Floyd Roberts, on pole. Behind them is Kelly Petillo. Pressing behind Petillo is intrepid Al Gordon. Alongside Gordon is Frank Wearne. Mays, in the "Winfield Special" Model-B Ford, went on to win the August 26, 1934 10-lap heat race.

Howdy Wilcox was among the outstanding drivers at Ascot and was for many years an entry in the Indianapolis 500. Wilcox died from natural causes .He's seated in this Miller in 1933 at Legion Ascot Speedway.

Sam Palmer was seriously burned in this Miller during a 1933 Ascot race. But Sam made a great comeback and drove creditably well.

Class B action. Ed Walker (No. 73) strikes Pinky Richardson's mount broadside during Ascot race in 1935. Richardson continued spinning out of the way and Walker went on to win consolation race.

Lane Curry, 1934, in the 'Riley Special." Curry got a late start at Ascot and departed for other tracks after Ascot's closure in January, 1936. His participation at the speedy oval was brief but a trying one. Curry was a half-brother to Ascot driver Jimmy Miller.

Frank Wearne, Ascot Speedway, 1934. Frank became an Indianapolis veteran driver after the closure of Ascot. Frank Kurtis built this car which ran on many other tracks.

Red Clark drove for Harry Jacquez and was an upcoming driver. He competed also in the Targo Floio, but lost his life on Ascot's north turn.

(Courtesy Roscoe Turner.)

One of the last pictures taken of famed Ernie Triplett, before his fatal crash, shows him putting on his famous red sweater for the last time. The ill-fated main event on the El Centro mile track in March, 1934, soon got underway. Al Gordon, extreme right, adjusts helmet before mounting the Sparks-Weirick Miller No. 1. Triplett was dead a few minutes later, the result of a four-car pileup. Eddie Offut (cap) watches.

(Doug Boyd collection)

Ernie Triplett lies dying in a cloud of dust on the El Centro mile dirt track. The terrible wreck also claimed the lives of driver Swede Smith and mechanic Hap Hafferly, who tried to pull Smith from the path of oncoming speeding racing cars. The race was stopped immediately, then resumed. Harb Balmer, in the "Gabhart Special," was declared the winner.

(Doug Boyd collection)

Mangled wreckage of what once was a beautiful racing car . . . aftermath of the fatal crash which claimed the life of Ernie Triplett in March 1934, at El Centro. Driver Swede Smith and Hap Hafferly, a mechanic, were also killed. Triplett carried No. 3 for placing third in the 1933 Coast title chase. Bill White's Miller was rebuilt, painted white and blue and was driven by Al Gordon during the remainder of 1934 and entire 1935.

(Doug Boyd collection.)

In 1934 Herb Balmer took Cliff Wilson's hot Miller for a spin and wound up over the Ascot fatal south turn fence. Although seriously injured, it wasn't long before Balmer was back in action. (Courtesy Roscoe Turner.)

Bob Austin drove Class A at Ascot and competed against such young "comers" as Ted Horn and George Robson. Because of his diligent and brilliant driving, Austin graduated into the "Big time" Class A field of drivers.

Harris Insinger gets victory kiss from Swedish woman race driver Greta Molander, after winning "Helmet Dash" at Ascot in 1935. The car is Russ Garnant's "Miller Special" No. 12.

Mel McKee receives Victory Crown from unidentified movie starlet. Legion Ascot Speedway, 1931.

Who set the fire? Some say the tramps, who slept underneath the grandstand's wooden tiers, set the blaze in vengence for loss of race driver friends. Pictured is entry way to Ascot offices, at rear of stands. The blaze erupted on April 27, 1936.

It didn't take long for flames to spread through Ascot's old grandstand. Firefighters worked fast to prevent total destruction. It didn't matter . . . the entire structure, built long ago by Jack Prince, soon yielded to wrecking crews.

Harris Insinger came from Philadelphia. He was graduated from Drexel Institute but chose auto racing as his profession. He died in 1935 on the Oakland mile after being a standout driver at Ascot.

Frank Wearne planted a heavy foot on racing cars at Ascot during the 1933-35 seasons, and was a constant threat to the likes of Rex Mays, Harris Insinger, Al Gordon, Louie Tomei, Floyd Roberts and Ray Pixley. He remained active for the next 15 years on tracks across the country. October 21, 1935.

An unidentified Ascot driver. Does anybody know? Is he Dewey Skipworth? Please someone, come forth with correct identification.

A tired Rex Mays smiles after winning a scorching 100-lap main event at Ascot. The car: the Art Sparks-Paul Weirick "Gilmore Special." April 25, 1935.

Ascot's closure to professional auto racing didn't prevent another fatality. On May 8, 1937, 16 months after being closed, youths took to the track in two cars to play racing driver—with fatal results. Mario Vega, 16, of Los Angeles, was killed when he was thrown from the Ford convertible. City engineers quickly dug many trenches across the track to keep other autos off, and prevent other such mishaps.

"Big Head" Sketches of Famous Ascot Drivers

(Drawn by Jack Buxton, 1928 Pacific Southwest Champion)

WALT MAY

AL GORDON

ARVOL BRUNMIER

KELLY PETILLO

NICK MARTINO

CHET GARDNER

GEORGE CONNOR

BILL CUMMINGS

BILL HEISLER

HERB BALMER

RALPH DE PALMA

LES SPANGLER

LOUIE MEYER

FRANK LOCKHART

JIMMY SHARP

LEON DURAY

PETE DE PAULO

REX MAYS

FRANCIS QUINN

TED HORN

ERNIE TRIPLETT

SHORTY CANTLON

DEWEY SKIPWORTH

WILBUR SHAW

CARL RYDER

BABE STAPP

SWEDE SMITH

MEL McKEE

SPEED HINKLEY

BOB CAREY

I REMEMBER ASCOT . . .

By Eddie Winfield

Ed Winfield's hopped-up Model-T had "wings" during Ascot early years. Driver Winfield built the speedster. Ed and his brother Bud later developed the famed Winfield downdraft carburetor. Ed was photographed on February 6, 1927.

Indianapolis and board track veteran Harry Hartz shakes the hand of Eddie Winfield after Ed won the "Helmet Dash" in December, 1927. The car is the "Kant-Score Special" hopped-up Model-T. At left is Sonny Guerke, owner of the first speed shop in Los Angeles. Hatless man is Glendale merchant John Lamulara. (Doug Boyd collection).

(See story next page)

"I was born in Pasadena and I became interested, as a 13-year-old, in racing at La Canada, Gardena and at Santa Maria. This was about 1916. My first racing car was a Model-T L-head engine which I drove at Hanford. That was a mile horse track.

"I had no particular idol whose footsteps I may have followed. As for the tracks, although I had no board track experience, I found the boards to be monotonous. Dirt and asphalt tracks, to me, were more exciting. There was more competition on dirt . . . there were many board drivers who couldn't drive on dirt.

"As for some of the earlier drivers, Eddie Pullen, Eddie Rickenbacker, Ralph DePalma and Barney Oldfield were tops. DePalma was as great as they came. Earl Cooper was good, but not as good as DePalma on dirt. Oldfield was not fussy . . . he would put his foot into it. . . .

"I rode as mechanic with Fred Frame in the first race Frame ever drove. That was at the original Ascot mile (Manchester and Central avenues, Los Angeles). I was 16 years old. I told them I was 21 years old and I became a registered 3-A mechanic.

"When Ascot off Valley Boulevard opened in 1924, I was not there as a driver but as a mechanic. I was putting on Winfield carbs on all the cars. I recall the main grandstand on the home straightaway on opening day. There was no racing in that area prior to 1924.

" (Frank) Lockhart won the first hillside course race . . . about 1925. There was no championship category before 1928. The American Legion had the most successful promotions there. Everybody else flunked it —Bon MacDougal, Harry Lutz, Alex Sloan, Harlan Fengler, George Bentel. They promoted outlaw races. (Dr. Fred) Loring had real class. He paved the track. (Dr. Loring, of American Legion Post 127, Glendale, California) .

"The Hooker Special No. 99 was a double overhead cam Miller. Shortly after its beginning, the track was closed for a while. When racing resumed I got numeral 1 on my car because I intended to be 'up there'. A number was just a number prior to 1928. Numeral 99 was the only number Harry Hooker ever used. Nobody wanted number 13. Bentel was the track's first promoter, but (publicist) Bill Pickens did all the work.

"Lockhart was a nice fellow . . . a good, young boy. He'd broadside the turns too much, but became one of the world's top drivers. Lockhart went faster than Benny Hill at Indianapolis. Pete Kreis became ill at Indy in 1926. I recommended Lockhart drive the Kreis car. Lockhart was a kid mechanic and terrific driver . . . he won the '26 race by about three miles.

"Harry Miller was a genius, but others did most of the work. Leo Goosen was by far the best man Miller ever had. Goosen was a great thinker and draftsman. My first carbs were either updraft or sidedraft. All the Miller carbs were replaced at Indianapolis in 1925 with my downdraft carburetors. These carbs were made originally for passenger cars. Henry Ford introduced cross springs on Model-T cars.

"As for Ascot, the fences were dangerous. Some drivers took unnecessary chances, but not all of them. Seems the drivers today are more daring and take more chances because they have more protection—crash helmets, roll bars, roll cages, fireproof coveralls.

"Wibur Shaw may have been the first driver to wear a regular crash helmet in U. S. competition (1932), but I wore a football helmet . . . that was about 1926. It became the joke of the day. I was criticized, laughed at, heckled. Any protection a driver used was considered chicken. The helmet was of hard leather used by football players during the 1920s. I didn't use it anymore, though. I was always for making cars safe. I had a steel brace inside the cowl . . . like a rollbar . . . it was reinforced under the cowl. I also used a steel steering wheel.

"As for horsepower on my Model-T, the valves, ports, cams and manifold compression ratio amounted to 200 horsepower. I could do 140 mph on a straight. I could go faster with a 6 to 1 compression ratio. My Model-T beat No. 99 in a match race which wound up as a 25-mile match race. I wanted a five-lap endurance race . . . a speed test. I beat 'em all the way.

"In the early 1930s they limited the cars at Ascot to 200 horsepower. This was due to the deaths. Their limit of one carburetor per car did no good. I decided to make a Model-B with rocker arm head. They called it the "Winfield Special" because I designed the head . . . designed it for publicity and to beat the Millers. This Model-B was on the same chassis as the earlier Hispano car driven by Rex Mays. Mays almost quit this car because it was no good. I saw problems in the exhaust pipes. The car had two exhaust pipes . . . two pipes overscavanged the engine. Rex was 1934 champ in this car.

"Tires weren't much problem when Ascot was dirt. More problems as an asphalt track. There would have been less accidents if kept as a dirt track. Harry Schmidt wanted me to be a star there, but I quit. Not enough time to drive the cars and maintain the cars too.

"Pop Evans was a driver and handled track maintenance. Pop wanted the track to be dirt, but the Legion wanted asphalt because of less maintenance. Dirt-oil mixture won out.

"Francis Quinn got all out of a car. He never lost a car . . . never did crazy things others do. He handled all kinds of situations. Quinn was quiet and reserved person . . . never said too much. A great driver . . . tough competitor. I rate Quinn higher than Triplett. Quinn did things as they should be done . . . a master of any situation. There were great duels between Quinn and Triplett. Ernie had the faster car and Quinn asked me for car improvements. Francis was one of the best drivers ever behind the wheel.

"Quinn built his new Miller and I was going to work on the car. But Francis had his highway accident and that was that. Triplett won the (1931) title in Bill White's car.

"I remember when cyclist Ray Wishart was killed at Ascot. I made Al Gordon famous. I recommended Al to Joe Petralli. Gordon was never headed thereafter . . . in 1933, I ground the camshafts and improved the Sparks-Weirick car. I recall Harry Jacques breaking his back. He drove the "Redlands Special". Bob Carey was a great dirt track driver. Bob's car was an 8-valve Miller. The Ascot north turn fence was of steel railing . . . a car was able to get under the railing. That fence was not properly designed. If you hit that fence you were done.

"Bill White was unsuccessful competing with Fords. Bill said (Harry) Miller would build him a 220. That didn't materialize. I got the 8-valve job instead with cams. I put in flat cups . . . ran better than the 16 valve block job . . . ran the car with 8 valves and flat cups.

(Art) Sparks' 16-valve job took over with Al Gordon driving. The car beat White's

8-valve job. My preference is a 4-valve job.

"Goosen worked for 55-cents per hour during the depression. Miller's day ended with the end of the board track era. Ascot was the proving ground for 4-cylinder engines. The supercharged and straight-8 car days were over. The 4-cylinder engine ran at Indianapolis because there was nothing else . . . they enjoyed longest run at Indy. Needed today is a new engine to compete with the Cosworth . . . could possibly improve the old Offy but we probably need a new engine.

"Back to the 1920s, there were no changes in engines . . . all were the same. But my carbs made important changes . . . changes from Miller carbs. DePalma was first to use my carbs at Indy. In 1935 Offenhauser adopted my cams as standard equipment. The CRA (California Racing Association) guys got 'free' information from me and I was advisor to the dragsters . . convinced them long ago to drive on rear wheels.

"My last race at Ascot was in 1927. I decided then to stick to development and providing parts for race cars. As for some of the other drivers at Ascot, Chet Gardner was a conservative driver, Bill Cummings was a good dirt driver. Wilbur Shaw was a reserved person and a gentleman . . . very nice fellow. Al Gordon was the hardest pusher, Quinn was a hard pusher. Francis had clean habits. He had irregular heartbeat . . . reason for his being barred from Indianapolis, but he drove all cars to their limit. Les Spangler was always in the headlines. Bill Spence took chances. Bill would say, 'I'm a fatalist . . . I'll get it when the time comes.' But I say, I know we'll all get it when the time comes, but no sense in pushing it.

"Shorty Cantlon was a throttle pusher. Jimmy Sharp hit his height of fame in 1929. As for Arvol Brunmier, he was a good, steady competitor . . . always in a spectacular happening . . . I recall his marriage at Ascot . . . right on the track.

"It's hard to say who was the best driver. Ralph DePalma was the first best one. Triplett, Gordon, Babe Stapp, Quinn, Lockhart, Sig Haugdahl . . . they were all great. Oh, and let's not forget "Stubby" Stubblefield, Mel Kenealy, George Souders, Johnny Krieger, Walt May, Charley Gelston, Bryan Saulspaugh, Kelly Petillo . . . they were all great.

"Leon Duray was also great . . . good as they came. Leon's 124 mph at Indianapolis in 1927 in that front-drive Miller is one of the greatest achievements. He was Ascot's villain."

ART SPARKS AND PAUL WEIRICK SAY "ASCOT WAS MOST DRAMATIC"

Paul Weirick works on the famed Sparks-Weirick car which holds the all-time Ascot lap record. At this time, the car was painted red and yellow, was called "Gilmore Special" and was driven by Rex Mays. Al Gordon won the 1933 title in this car, Mays was 1935 champ in same race car.

Gold toothed "Stubby" Stubblefield is flanked by Paul Weirick (left) and Art Sparks in this 1931 picture taken at the Legion Ascot Speedway. Sparks and Weirick built the famed "Sparks-Weirick Miller Special" (or "Poison Lil") which set the all-time Ascot lap record with Al Gordon the driver. "Stubby" was killed in the 1935 Indianapolis time trials. (Art Sparks Collection.)

(See story next page)

(Art Sparks and Paul Weirick built the "Miller Special" racing car in which Al Gordon set the all-time Ascot lap record of 25:43 seconds in 1933).

"I remember Ascot as being the best track in the world for the spectator . . . you could sit anywhere in the grandstand and see the whole race," said Sparks.

"Ascot provided the stiffest competition of any race course . . . the drivers were the best in the country . . . many who took unbelievable chances, and who yielded nothing to his competitor," said Weirick.

"For competitive racing . . . don't forget, the spectators determine the success of a track . . . I saw the stands full where nobody could get in . . . week after week. Competition and evenness of the races gave the people what they wanted," Sparks recalled.

Sparks continued, "I don't think anybody got a better show than those who attended Ascot races.

"There was no better grade of car than the one on the first row to the one at the back. They all had good shocks, good axles and tires . . . the best of everything.

"The equipment was good . . . no better grade of cars than those at Ascot. In the last 10 years I saw cars at Indianapolis that were in far worse shape than those in Ascot's heyday."

Weirick has high praise for Ernie Triplett. He says, "There may have been drivers competing earlier who were considered better, but Triplett, to me, was as good as any. Given an equal car, you were up against a tough man in Triplett. It boils down to the best car-man combination.

"Rex Mays, Kelly Petillo and Al Gordon were also very good. I wasn't in competition with Francis (Quinn), so it's hard for me a compare Quinn with Ernie."

Said Sparks, "There were plenty of good drivers—Quinn, Lester Spangler, Bryan Saulspaugh, but Mays was endoctrinated right away. He drove western cars . . . knew what the score was. Gordon came from fire engine days . . . seems he drove a car that always caught fire. Yet, Quinn was one of the best . . . he was tops during the 20's when we came along."

Sparks continued, "Jimmy Sharp was the only driver that ever got killed, hurt or maimed driving for us. He got killed at Oakland . . . we don't know what happened. Paul and I went over that car with a fine tooth comb and we found nothing wrong with the car, although somebody said the steering wheel broke."

As for Eastern drivers, Sparks said, "Lou Moore came out to Ascot but didn't do much. Mauri Rose came out with a two-cam Fronty . . . he had all the credentials in the world, but he did very little. There was always animosity between Eastern and Western drivers at Ascot. The Eastern hotdogs who drove at Roby, Indianapolis and at Langhorne just couldn't get around Ascot worth a damn. The best Eastern driver was Bill Cummings. "Wild Bill" was colorful, talented and spectacular.

"Cliff Bergere was an Eastern driver who could keep a car off the fence, but he scared hell out of us. I told Cliff a few years ago, 'You're the best driver going backwards we ever had.' "

Weirick recalls Ascot promotions under American Legion Post 127 as "the best in the country." The Legion demanded perfection, said Weirick, stating, "The Legion was always on the up and up."

Sparks also had praise for the Legion. "The Legion had good, clean shows. We could never chisel a dime out of them.

"We were sorry when the Legion bowed out in 1934 . . . guess too many guys were getting killed," Sparks went on. "Yet, I doubt that this was the reason for the Legion's bow-out.

"As for Ascot's closure we're sorry it

Doug Boyd, who lives in Burbank, California, taught metalshop at Woodrow Wilson High School in Los Angeles.

When Boyd wasn't teaching the art of working with metal, he occupied himself by restoring vintage racing cars, collecting old racing car parts, building a street hop-up of his own and reliving the glorious past of Legion Ascot Speedway.

Boyd has collected Ascot momentos for several years, lived not far from where the track situated and keeps in contact with old racing car drivers and mechanics.

Furthermore, Wilson High is located just over the hill from where old Ascot existed.

Recently Boyd told some students that not far from the field where the Wilson football team plays its games, a famous auto racing track was operated by the American Automobile Association and Post 127 of the Glendale American Legion. Here's what he told them:)

"If, while sitting in the crisp night air watching the mighty Mules score, you might chance to think that these hills have never before heard such an uproar.

"Well forget it kids. Whether you know it or not they have.

Forty-six years ago 16,000 to 25,000 people twice weekly rocked these knolls but good as the roar of 15 to 25 open exhaust race cars streaked across what roughly now is Yellowstone, Vineburn, Catalpa and Jones (or Boca) streets at speeds as high as 120 miles per hour! Our field is built on the hill that used to be called "Pikers Peak" where spectators who could not afford the price of a ticket sat in the grass to watch the spectacle below. Mr. Eshom's (teacher) front lawn was part of the treacherous north turn of the 5/8 mile killer course.

The track known as Ascot Speedway was opened Thanksgiving Day 1924 and continued until 1936 when the 21st man was killed and public indignation erupted a storm of controversy between the racers and the press. The track was closed and after the grandstand mysteriously burned down one week later, the track never reopened.

"The men who raced at Ascot Speedway, later called Legion Ascot when it was sponsored by Post 127 of the American Legion, were men of steel nerves. These daredevils wore no crash helmets, only cloth "Snoopy-type" helmets and goggles, had no roll bars and only two wheel brakes for hair-raising speeds up to 120, their elbows sticking out in the breeze unprotected. These were depression times and young men found the lure of instant riches all too tempting. For 21 it cost them their lives.

"Some of the great drivers were Ed Winfield, Mel Kenealy, Francis Quinn, Al Gordon, Rex Mays, Ernic Triplett, "Wild Bill" Cummings Kelly Petillo, Frank Lockhart, "Stubby" Stubblefield, Babe Stapp, Floyd Roberts, Ralph DePalma, Fred Frame, Jimmy Sharp and Wilbur Shaw. These names, still famous today in the facing circles, fill the hall of fame of auto racing. All drove here and most are dead by now."

Boyd said he visited Ed Winfield, now 80 and living in Las Vegas. He had many interesting stories to tell as he was the No. 1 driver at Ascot in 1926 and 1927, racing his home built Model-T modified that turned an incredible 132 miles an hour at the Beverly Hills board track that same year.

The drivers were not the only famous people attending the events, for it was really 'the place' to go in Southern California on Sunday afternoons or Wednesday nights. Movie stars galore attended regularly and you could usually see motion picture personalities sitting in the lower boxes dressed in their finest. Even the race drivers and mechanics wore ties and were scrupulously dressed as were the officials in their uniforms of black sweaters over white dress shirts with bow ties, white linen golfing trousers (knickers) trimmed with high black and white checkered socks.

The motion picture regulars were Joan Blondell, Constance Bennett, Doug Fairbanks, Jr., heavyweight boxing champ Jack Dempsey, world champion wrestler Ed "Strangler" Lewis, "Cotton" Warburton of USC football fame, Jack Oakie, Charlie Chaplin, Wallace Beery, Loretta Young, Clara Bow, William Powell and many others.

"I was only 7 or 8," Boyd recalled, "when my older sister's boyfriend piled me into his ancient open 1925 Star touring car and drove me to the track over Monterey Road from Eagle Rock where we lived. I had never been so excited by anything in my young life, and can't ever forget the smell of the burning castor oil used to lubricate those early engines, and the sound of those roaring exhausts.

"I've been a racing buff ever since the first day at the Legion Ascot Speedway."

Asked why there is no evidence of the next most famous track America has ever produced (Indianapolis Speedway is the most famous), Boyd commented, "Auto racing fell out of good graces with the press in the early days when so many drivers lost their lives.

"Auto racing is still very big in South America and Europe where fans outnumber all other sports with the exception of soccer.

"I really feel it's a shame that some of the streets at the old Ascot site are not named after the great drivers who lived and died heroically upon those oil soaked grounds. Yellowstone should be "Triplett's Terrace," Vineburn "Mays Avenue," Jones "Gordon Grove," Catalpa "Pasa DePalma," Multnomah "Ascot Drive," and maybe a "Quinn Circle." He added laughing, "but who's going to ask an 8-year-old?"

TALKIN' WITH . . .

"BURN 'EM UP BARNES"

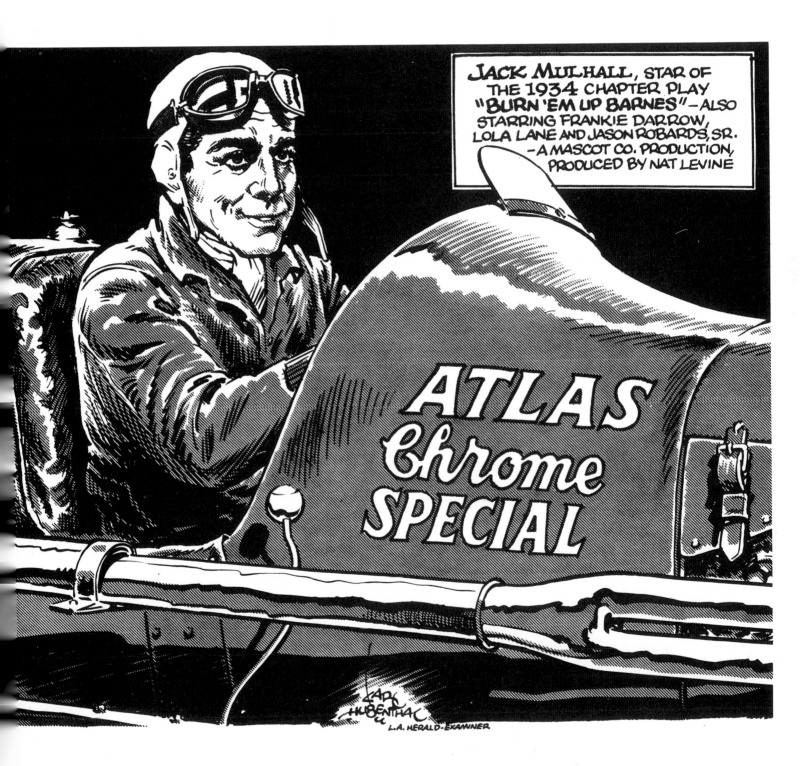

JACK MULHALL, STAR OF THE 1934 CHAPTER PLAY "BURN 'EM UP BARNES" — ALSO STARRING FRANKIE DARROW, LOLA LANE AND JASON ROBARDS, SR. — A MASCOT CO. PRODUCTION, PRODUCED BY NAT LEVINE

ATLAS Chrome SPECIAL

L.A. HERALD-EXAMINER

(A combination of the "Atlas Chrome Special" driven by Ted Horn at Ascot and used in the film, the style of goggles worn by Wilbur Shaw, and a picture of Jack Mulhall, himself, produced this sketch by Los Angeles Herald-Examiner staff artist Karl Hubenthal.)

(Author's note: Jack Mulhall passed away at the Woodland Hills motion picture retirement home in 1980.)

Veteran Hollywood actor Jack Mulhall, who starred in the 12-chapter serial play "Burn 'em Up Barnes" which was filmed at Ascot in 1934, remembers the old track as "having a great reputation for entertainment and racing."

The 90-year-old actor, star of countless "thrill" films for decades and who today resides at the Motion Picture and Television Country House in Woodland Hills, California, added more recall about the track:

"It seems like the drivers at Ascot would take more chances than they do now. It was an old and dangerous track . . . it was a thrill just to go there.

"Most of the drivers competed there because it was sort of a Roman Holiday. It was rare when a race was ran where there wasn't some sort of a spectacular accident.

"Ascot sort of reminded me of a Roman Holiday . . . I've been to the Colosseum in Rome and I've walked past the warriors' dressing room there.

"The drivers at Ascot reminded me of those warriors.

"Ascot had night racing which always was a thrill. There were many accidents and a lot of the fellas got hurt . . . even killed.

"I remember one chap being killed there. I remember giving him an opal pin. I remember because that's my birth stone.

"I asked him if he was superstitious and he said 'no.' When he had his accident, they found the stickpin ground into the floorboard and it was crushed."

The character, "Burn 'em Up Barnes," was created by a well-known comedian named Johnny Hines, who starred in the silent version, Mulhall related. However, he added, producer Nat Levine of the Mascot Co., converted the silent film into a talkie. The picture was "shot" partly at Republic Studios.

The 12-chapter serial, besides Mulhall as "Burn 'em Up," also starred the beautiful Lola Lane, Frankie Darro and the legendary Jason Robards, Sr., all of whom were hand-picked by Levine, Mulhall recalled.

Of course, Ascot's "Knights of the Roaring Road" participated in the "action" shots.

"My salary for starring in the film was about $1,500 a week. I was guaranteed 10 weeks of work and we completed the picture in about nine weeks. We worked 14 or 15 hours per day until the film was completed," he said.

Was that you or a racing driver behind the wheel of the "Atlas Chrome Special" flashing through the turns and down the straightaways? he was asked.

"That was me. I had to do most of the driving, including stunts of crashing through board fences and running off the track. That's what I was getting paid for. But I never got hurt filming "Burn 'em Up Barnes."

"The Atlas Chrome Special," driven at Ascot by Ted Horn, was purchased outright by Nat Levine for the film. But we used mostly Ascot racing films in the backdrop because we couldn't afford to purchase all those cars to make the film.

"At times, I went fairly fast, but most of the time they sped up the camera to protect me and the other people involved in the film making.

"I had to be careful. A lapse of memory or poor judgment could have resulted in me being killed or some decent citizen as well.

"Making the film was a very busy time. We'd work until late at night sometimes.

"Film making was dangerous, too. Republic films invested the money and they took every precaution to protect the actors.

"That scene atop the grandstand from where I 'fell,' well, they placed a mattress on the ground on which I tumbled after fighting with that 'heavy' and the timber high on the grandstand 'broke.'

"The fact that you watched us film that episode . . . you as a little tike . . . is a kick I'm getting now . . . knowing that you were there . . . and so long ago.

"You're right, I swung from a hanging piece of timber and I fell four or five feet onto the mattress to break the 'fall,' but film techniques made it appear that I fell from way above. That was a dummy falling, or course. Anything could have happened . . . we had to be careful. Sometimes we were actually hit by a 'heavy's' blow. Sometimes you don't know the other guy's strength. I'd fight four or five 'heavies' at times," said Mulhall.

Did "Burn 'em Up Barnes" make any money for the company?

"The film made the actors rich and it also made Nat Levine rich, that's for sure, because he continued to make pictures long after "Burn 'em Up" had gone into limbo.

"I enjoyed making the film. I always enjoyed working. It's exciting because you do a lot of exciting things. I always enjoyed speed because it was competitive."

Do you enjoy seeing yourself in a motion picture?

"I'm a great Mulhall fan," he chuckled.

Mulhall said he first saw clips of "Burn 'em Up Barnes" in the studio, but saw it entirely when it was presented to the public.

"Today we hear about "Burn 'em Up Barnes" from all over the world. The picture is a big hit in the Orient, particularly in Japan. It had a great reception in Manila, too . . . like many places where they like a lot of action, such as in the Philippine Islands."

Mulhall had this to say about the film's other stars:

Jason Robards—"He was a fine, legitimate actor . . . the brutal 'heavy' in "Burn 'em Up Barnes." It was a pleasure to work with him. In fact, the whole crew was wonderful and everybody connected with the organization."

Frankie Darro—"Little Frankie Darro was such a wonderful kid to work with. He was very alert, very smart and a very competent and capable artist. His dad was a competent acrobat in vaudeville. Frankie was a very capable stuntman, himself. He was very good with automobiles and was very cooperative."

Lola Lane—"She was delightful to co-star with. Sometimes she'd get a little nervous. When you're making a hurry-up picture you've got to hustle and think and do it while you're talking. I'd help calm her down by suggesting how to go about things. It was pure joy working with her."

He continued, "Over all, we didn't have much time to rehearse "Burn 'em Up Barnes." Everything was done at a speed-up tempo. For instance: 'come on, get in there, come on, get on with it . . . never mind if your leg hurts.'"

After 43 years, there I was, speaking to "Burn 'em Up" himself. I am 51 and Jack Mulhall is 90. Yet, I can recall when I was very young and he a matured man of 47 and filming the epic "Burn 'em Up Barnes" at Ascot.

"Well, it's great to be remembered," Jack Mulhall said, bowing religiously, as I left the Woodland Hills retirement home.

"The Crowd Roars"

A Warner Bros. Production

"Speed demons with goggled eyes glued on glory—grinning at death—laughing at love, breaking necks to break records, while the crowd roars for blood.

"Never, never, NEVER has the screen shown such nerve wracking action lifted right off the track of the world's greatest speedway.

"It's the thrill epic of all time . . . the talk of every town that's seen it.

"Forty men risked death to film it. Miss it at your own risk . . ."

It's Joe Greer behind the wheel of the "Greer Special." You're wrong, friend, it's actor James Cagney, who portrayed "Joe Greer" in the 1931 Warner Brothers production, "The Crowd Roars." Filmed at Ascot, the action melodrama also starred Joan Blondell, Ann Dvorak, Guy Kibbee, Frank McHugh, Eric Linden, Regis Toomey and a host of Ascot drivers.

Stars in the Ascot action epic "The Crowd Roars," are from left: Eric Linden, Joan Blondell, James Cagney and Ann Dvorak. The Warners motion picture was filmed at Ascot in 1931.

Actor James Cagney visited driver Bryan Saulspaugh in the infield on March 2, 1932, soon after release of the Warner Brothers racing epic "The Crowd Roars," in which Cagney played the leading role. Alongside Cagney is driver Lou Moore. The car is Danny DePaolo's Miller.

This car, built by Carl Mikkelsen, had a half (4 cylinder) of a Hisso aircraft engine. It competed respectably in Ascot night races. Mikkelsen is in the car; its regular driver during 1935 was Frenchy La Horgue, at Carl's side.

Do You Remember? When... a few years ago!

—"Stubby" drove the fast little No. 18 for Russ Garnant and for a good many races showed the boys the short way around the track. (Yes, girls, that is a mustache and we remember the day his "ma" gave him heck or something for using all of her eyebrow pencil trying to make it black).

—"Shorty" Cantlon was driving for Bill White in the Miller No. 16. We understand Bill's new car will be with us tonight with Kelly at the wheel. "Shorty" is still in the East, but he and his crew are heading West in a few weeks. We know a good many of his fans will be on hand to greet him when he arrives.

—Kelly Petillo in Car No. 40 when he was leading the field in one of our first long races (100 laps) and had just three laps to go when the axle broke. That's what you call hard luck. The next race he was driving the Tri-Flex special, had the fastest qualifying time, won the Helmet Dash, and again broke up.—That's dammsite more hard luck.—We hope that tonight he has lost some of his bad luck.

—Johnny Krieger drove the Western Super Special for Charlie Caraba (standing by car). That was a real team, but the real manager of the team sat in the grandstand. If you have not already guessed it was Mrs. Johnny "Ma" Krieger. "Ma" knows as much if not more about race cars and motors than her husband. (We understand that Johnny is building a new car, and will be with us soon and so will "Ma").

It's "Poison Lil" in 1950. Art George is at the wheel at Wausau, Wisconsin's half mile dirt track. The car was built in 1931 by Art Sparks and Paul Weirick. The "Gilmore Special" was driven to the 1933 AAA championship by Al Gordon. The car's first drivers were "Stubby" Stubblefield and Arvol Brunmeier. The car later was painted red and yellow and Rex Mays drove it to the 1935 championship. Joe Gemsa of El Monte, California, currently owns the car.

Restoring Racing Cars for Posterity

(How They Look Today...)

(Richard Rose photo)

(Richard Rose photo)

Right Joe Gemsa is seated in the "Dayton Thorobred Special", the car which was driven to the Pacific Coast Championship in 1930 by Francis Quinn. Quinn, of course, drove the "Gabhhart Special" Fronty Ford, along with the Dayton, enroute to the title. Your author stands alongside Gemsa's pride.

(Mike Sergieff)

Left: The "Deulin Special" is owned by Hank Becker of Garden Grove, California. Becker is in the car at the Baylands Raceway half mile dirt track during a Western Racing Association meet. The engine is a double overhead cam 1926 Ford T-block. Oldtime Ascot driver Earl Mansell once said, "I raced against it at least 100 times. It was fast for a T block and was in many trophy and Helmet Dashes. The problem was it had to run against all the "A" cars because of the double overhead cam engine, and it broke often, before the end of the race." Some say the car is a replica, or a facsimile of the original which was built by Guy Deulin. Whatever, the car carries on its side the names of its previous drivers at Ascot: "Stubby" Stubblefield, Guy Deulin, Walt May and Nick Martino.

Upper Left: Tim McHenry, of Canoga Park, received this "gift of appreciation"-Harry Hooker's famous Model-T rocket, from Lindley Bothwell of Woodland Hills. Bothwell bought the car from Hooker's wife in 1957 at Phoenix, Arizona. McHenry began restoration in 1960 for Bothwell in Canoga Park. It's an original beauty. Upper Center: Joe Ricker of Anaheim, put together this 490 single overhead cam beauty. The car carries a 1925 Chevrolet engine. It's said Kelly Petillo drove this car at Ascot. Upper Right: Jim Lattin, a Pomona resident, purchased this car in Florida in May, 1987. It's a two cam double overhead Cragar. Restored in Florida, the car originally had a 220 cubic inch Miller. At a recent Oldtimer's meet at Ascot Park in Gardena, it was mentioned among some oldsters that this car was driven at Ascot by Chet Gardner. (Richard Rose photo)

Left: Kenny Howard (big black hat), and his refined "Winfield Special." In the car is its creator-Paul Fromm, who, with Clyde Adams, built this car. The head was designed by Ed Winfield, of course. Rex Mays copped the 1934 Pacific Coast AAA title in this car. Ascot driver Jack Taylor shakes hands with admirer; Carl Schmidt (the "walnut man"), at rear.

Right: Bob Drollinger admires his beautiful "Gilmore Special" which was built by Roy Richter in 1936. It's an overhead valve job with Winfield cams; its wheelbase is 90 inches. This car was drive at Winchester, Indiana, by legendary Rex Mays. Drollinger is a West Los Angeles resident.

(Richard Rose photo)

The "Jackman Special" plowed the barrier along the home stretch in the late 1920s. Skip O'Connor lost a leg in the wreck. This car was also driven by Bill Bundy at that time.

It was trophy presentation time at Ascot in 1932. Left to right: Art Sparks, co-builder (with Paul Weirick) of the famed "Sparks-Weirick Special," which won the Coast title in 1933. Chet Gardner, runner-up for 1931 Coast honors. Les Spangler, who fractured his arm in a smash-up at Oakland. Far right is Ernie Triplett, 1931-32 Coast champion.

Carl Mikkelsen (in car) built this Model-T front drive in Hollywood about 1924 or 1925. Mikkelsen drove the car only once-at Bakersfield. His first driver was Hap Stelk.

Pacific Coast champ Ernie Triplett participated in this gag shot - a cigar in his chops. Actually, Ernie was a non-smoker; his exhaust pipe did the smoking for him. Bill White, owner of the Miller speedster on which Ernie is seated, offers a pensive expression.

Ed Winfield was famous for developing carburetors and camshafts. Winfield supplied such for many drivers at Ascot, at Indianapolis and at other tracks throughout the country. Here he applies an expert's touch.

Proving that haste makes waste, or something, here's Wilbur Shaw's car (side view), just after it had side-swiped Al Gordon's No. 23, which is aimed the wrong way. Gordon can be seen tumbling out on his head, while the right rear wheel on Shaw's car is shown declaring its independence. The crack-up took place on the 152nd lap. Ernie Triplett (1) and Stubby Stubblefield (9) whiz by.

The races are over... let them in!! Kids, and more kids, spill onto the Ascot track to see their favorite driver and racing car. The author recalls the many times he did the same thing. Fans would mill around the cars and drivers until sundown, or when management locked the gates.

The office of the Legion Ascot Speedway was located in the Arcade Building, between Fifth and Sixth streets, and between Spring Street and Broadway. Look closely and you can see the "big head" sketches, by Jack Buxton, of Petillo, Quinn, Cummings, Triplett, Kenealy, Sharp, Cantlon, Gelston, Hinkley, Heisler and Swede Smith.

Jimmy Wilkinson at the wheel of this creation. Frank Kurtis built this baby, which ran also at Silvergate Speedway in San Diego, at Oakland and El Centro... among other tracks. Besides Wilkinson, other notable drivers of this machine were Ted Horn and Ed Haddad. Its colors were red with black trim. The year: 1935.

Back straightaway action - at the Legion Ascot Speedway in 1933. Kelly Petillo, who won the '35 Indy race, is on the outside, while Mel Kenealy, in Earl Haskell's classy Miller No. 18, zooms by in the inside. Mel won this one. The author recalls standing alongside the No. 18 in 1933; the night program had ended and me and my older brother, Joe, wound up astride the car along the infield pits.

Ernie Triplett, two-time winner of the Pacific Coast, is here holding a model of his car, made by one of his rabid fans, Marchey Ayres of Los Angeles. It is an exact reproduction of the "Blond Terror's" car, even to having a miniature motor.

Francis Quinn and Claude French built this Miller Marine in 1930, the year that Francis won the Pacific Coast AAA title. Seated is Chris Vest, a prominent driver. Alongside is Earl Evans. The car is the original "Francis Quinn Special" which was stored in Ray Rapp's garage on Sichel Street and North Broadway in Lincoln Heights. Its original color was pale blue and gold numeral No. 1. Quinn, who died in a highway accident, drove the car sparingly, after its "christening" on the Ascot home stretch, attended by driver Walt May and Quinn's bride-to-be Gertrude Allen.

Lanky Ernie Triplett displays a lengthy trophy, presented to him after a big win at Ascot in 1931. The lady? Why, that's Ernie's wife-Lillian Hughes Triplett. She admires her husband with a loving smile. Who are those other guys? Ernie was enroute to his first Pacific Coast AAA championship.

Ray Dashbrook is shown broadsliding as he enters the south turn at Ascot. It's a Saturday practice day about 1932. Does anybody have information regarding this race car, and its driver?

Daredevil Bill Spence was a barnstorming airplane rider and pilot as well as a terrific race driver. A "Helmet Dash" win this time at Ascot in 1927. The "Hooker Special" was a most hairy race car in its era. Tim McHenry, of Canoga Park, California, is owner of this perfectly restored machine today. Spence died at Indy in 1929.

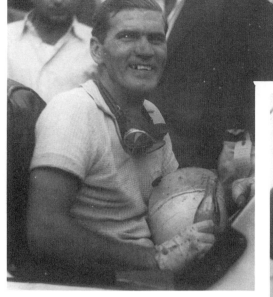

Ray Pixley was killed at Roby, Illinois, in 1936. Pixley, a Ascot standout driver, was born in Pasadena. This is Pixley after a Ascot feature win. Standing behind the ledfoot is Joe Zottarelli, who today resides in La Canada.

Hal Cole, right, and Ray Pixley chit-chat with an unidentified car owner, just before qualification proceedings began during an Ascot program. Pixley took his "last ride" at Roby in 1936. Cole was active in the big car circuit through 1949.

Roy Russing flipped this car over the Ascot south turn, resulting in a bevy of mechanics, car owners and pit crewmen to converge upon the scene on the hilly downslide of the treacherous south turn. Russing escaped with minor injuries.

Two hundred laps of grind on Ascot's dirt-oil surface... the cars are lined up and ready to roar. Mostly Millers... at 115 miles-per-hour down the straights and into the turns, they are: Wilbur Shaw, on the pole, and Chet Gardner on the outside (No. 2). Behind Shaw is Ernie Triplett and on the outside is Mel Kenealy (7). Behind Mel is Bill Cummings in Art Sparks' No. 6. Following are Babe Stapp, Carl Ryder, Louie Tomei, Shorty Cantlon and Sam Palmer. Triplett won the scorcher after Gordon, Gardner and Shaw tangled in two separate accidents.

Jack Petticord after winning a race at Ascot in the late 1920s. The lady in plume, presumably, is Jack's wife. However, despite efforts, this has not been confirmed. Who are the youngsters?

A racing program in 1931 found Jack taylor in competition. Here he is ready to qualify in his single overhead Fronty Ford. Beverly Brandon leans on car.

Rex Mays refreshes himself with a soft drink after winning a race at Ascot. Next to him is Augie Kent. Paul Fromm, builder of this Hispano ("Hisso Special") is at right. Man on left is unidentified. Mays provided stiff competition to Al Gordon and Ernie Triplett in this car during the 1933 title chase.

Paul Fromm built the Hispano-Suiza (Hisso) speedster in his Montrose garage. Rex Mays drove this car to dizzy heights and was immediate stiff competition to the faster Millers, particularly those of Al Gordon and Ernie Triplett.

Wilbur Shaw's car rests after sideswiping Al Gordon's car, which caused Chet Gardner to wind up upside down on the south turn. Shaw escaped with minor cuts and bruises, as did Gardner. Triplett went on to win the 200 lapper.

This wheel went airborne and into the stands amid the roar of the crowd at Ascot. Ernie Triplett, Bill Cummings and Chet Gardner were known to have thrown wheels similarly, but whose car this one belonged to is a mystery. An alert photographer was fortunate to ''catch'' the wheel. Was anybody hurt?

Mel McKee in the ''Burd Piston Ring Special'' at Ascot. Owner Carl Mikkelsen stands alongside.

It's Monday, February 12, 1934. Roy Russing took a dipsey-doodle on Ascot's treacherous south turn. Russing was not hurt during this afternoon's scheduled racing program. The guy standing alongside looks like Red Clark; any objections?

Rex Mays wins the "Helmet Dash" once again. It's 1935. Lois Wilson made the Victory Crown presentation. The car is the Sparks-Weirick creation which Al Gordon drove to the 1933 title. The car was painted Gilmore colors for 1935-red and yellow. It had Persian blue and silver numeral when Gordon drove it two years before.

Ascot aces talk things over. Nick Martino, right, refers to an item in the racing program. Francis Quinn, 1931 Coast champ, in center. George Young, the ill-fated Milwaukee driver, at left. Young lost his life in a four-car wreck in 1931. Quinn also died that year in a highway accident. Martino died the following year while "demonstrating" a hop-up in a school yard.

Mrs. Ernie Triplett (the former Lillian Hughes), poses proudly with daughter Doreen. The trophies, of course, are among the many won by the great champion.

There weren't very many empty seats when the Ascot aces took to the track. This was the typical scene on a Sunday afternoon, when the American Legion and the AAA put on the usual sensational show. Ascot's grandstand could seat 12,000.

Paul Durkham was the first-ever flagman at Ascot, being brought in from Bakersfield, to direct the track's first race on January 20, 1924. Durkham, who also promoted races at Bakerfield, was imported for the special event. Durkham later served Ascot as referee, timekeeper and pit boss.

"Getting Out Here!" was Sam Palmer's shout, as he jumped from his burning Miller. The car caught fire after a piston blew on the north turn at the fabulous Legion Ascot Speedway in 1932.

The "Foothill Special" was produced out of a Los Angeles garage. It was a Fronty Ford; in the cockpit is Dewey Skipworth. It's 1930 at the Ascot track. Skipworth was a cousin to "Woody" Woodford, a counterpart race driver at the legendary track in the Alhambra-Lincoln Heights area.

They Etched a Trail of Speed During

OTTO WOLFER

JOHNNY McDOWELL

JIMMY MILLER

JIMMY WILKINSON

H.D. PROVAN

FRED WINNAI

Ascot's Glorious, Exciting Years

OLIVER OBERG

AL PUTNAM

FREDDIE LYONS

TEX PETERSEN

AL REINKE

SAM ROSS

M.V. ROYAN

RALPH KINGSLEY

MIKE MOODY

BOB BULLOCK

CHARLEY FLETCHER

GEORGE HOWARD

GEORGE BECK

O.K. HUNSAKER

HARRY GENTRY

CARL KING BRADY

PAUL BARRETT

BERT FISHER

AL WALTERS

JIMMY KEMP

PETE NIELSEN

DAVE BUTLER

NICK NICHOLAS

BILLY WYNN

GUY DUELIN

BILL LIPSCOMB

BOB GRAGG

JACK TAYLOR

HERMAN SCHURCH

CLARENCE DOWNING

ROY RUSSING

BARNEY KLEOPFER

CLIFF WILSON

LOUIE WEBB

HUGH SCHUCK

ART SCOVELL

VIC FELT

ED WALKER

STAN HALLETT

AL HOPP

TOMMY COSMAN

This was the "last resting place" for Harry Jacques' racing car when, because of a blowout, it hurtled the fence on the south turn on a Wednesday night race. Although the car was a total loss, Jasques escaped with only head cuts. To the layman it appears an impossibility to mend the car, but ingenious mechanics had it rebuilt for the following night racing show.

Bob Scovel in his Rajo Special at Ascot. Scovel, a Portlander, drove remarkably well in Ascot competition from 1929 to 1931.

Babe Stapp's garage (call it a fillin' station), was the centerpoint, or should we say, the gathering point of the racing stars of the day. Babe's Stapp Pit'' was located on South Flower Street at 16th Street in Los Angeles, on the northwest corner. There is where the race drivers of the day-Cummings, Petillo, Shaw, Carey, Triplett, Gordon, Spangler, Brunmier, Gardner, Connor, Cole, Stubby, Brentlinger and so many others would congregate. The Miller (inset), appears to be that of Harvey Ward, the car in which Brunmeir set the all-time ''night'' lap record at Ascot.

Wreckage of H.D. (Hal) Provan's car is hauled from the backstretch after his fatal accident on Sept. 18, 1932. Provan's car, the ''Y Service Special,'' hit the backstretch fence, shot 25 feet into the air and burst into flames.

"Speed"

Roared at Ascot During the Roarin' Twenties

Byron "Speed" Hinkley was born at Elba, Nebraska, on Oct. 28, 1898.

He spent his youth on his father's farm, where he did regular farming chores, including helping dad Bill Hinkley repair farm equipment, trucks and family autos.

"Dad was a good mechanic and he helped me build my first racing car—a Buick passenger car which we converted into a racer. That was about 1918. I used that car for racing on half mile tracks of the midwest and I also used it as a passenger car," said Hinkley.

Hinkley said he drove his first race at Corning, Nebraska, and also raced on half milers at Lincoln, at St. Paul (Nebraska), and also ran the county fair circuits in Nebraska and Kansas.

"Most of the tracks were half milers and most of the races were twenty-five lappers," Hinkley added.

The years have sapped his memory for the most part, but did recall moving with his family to Pasadena. "We came out west about 1920," he said. We opened a repair shop in Pasadena.

Besides working in his dad's auto repair shop, Hinkley resumed his racing career in California.

His lapsing memory recalls few racing details, but did remember dueling with Francis Quinn, Babe Stapp, Walt May and Fred Frame.

"I really can't recall" was his reply to many questions seeking answers.

However, he remembers racing at Ascot, Fresno Bakersfield, San Luis Obispo and at San Jose. Ascot and San Jose were five-eights mile tracks, the other three were full mile dirt ovals.

Hinkley had dumped the old Buick and had "graduated" to Rajos, Fronty Fords and other creations, including Ted Simpson's 1 2-cylinder Chrysler.

"Speed" was asked if he was ever hurt in a race; you guessed it: "I just can't recall," was his reply.

Top to bottom: Hinkley at age 90 in 1988. He was residing in the Azusa Mountains, about two miles from the city.)

Hinkley in Ted Simpson's powerful 12-cylinder Chrysler.

Hinkley leads unidentified drivers out of north turn.

Hinkley leads Fred Frame.

Speed sits proudly in Cecil Bellanger's "Bellanger Rajo" after winning Helmet Dash.

Francis Quinn, Babe Stapp, Hinkley, left to right.

Speed in Pasadena car dealer Leon Kingsley's "Kingsley Special."

Driver Curley Young put on a gag in this one-dressed like a woman-cigar and all. Al's Auto Shop was sponsor of this Fronty in 1930. Who are the guys standing alongside?

Right: Three-time Indy winner Louie Meyer is seated in this eight-cylinder Miller at Ascot in 1930. "This is the only car I drove at Ascot, which I owned. I had minimal success with it," said Meyer, from his home in Searchlight, Nevada.

Left: Babe Stanyer, 25 years old at this time, was a very ambitious race driver. Babe, who hailed from Alhambra, California, was fatally injured on October 29, 1933, when his car blew a tire and plunged over the south turn fence. Stanyer, far back in the field, rocketed over the fence on the seventh lap during a 15-lap consolation race. He died enroute to White Memorial Hospital.

The Vai brothers, John, left, and Jim, right, of Cucamonga, California, display their wares-the Victory Crown Helmet-created in honor of the great Ralph DePalma. The helmet was presented to the winner of the "Helmet Dash" which featured a two-lap race between the two fastest qualifiers-the first race of the day's (or night) program. Later, this race featured the three fastest qualifiers. The Vai brothers, owners of a Cucamonga winery, created the helmet in honor of their countryman DePalma. The helmet today is valued at $15,000.

Al Gordon, 1933 Pacific Coast champion, reviews scrapbook illustrating old rivals, with his son, Al, Jr. This picture "ran" in the old L.A. Daily News the day after Gordon's fatal crash in Ascot's final race on January 25, 1936. Riding Mechanic Spider Matlock perished in the same crash on the south turn.

Louie Schneider, as a youthful driver at Ascot. Schneider came to Ascot in the late 1920s. Louie made steady progress which led to his winning the 1931 Indianapolis race.

Hal Cole and his beautiful Miller at the Legion Ascot Speedway in 1934. Cole, along with Floyd Roberts, George Connor and Ray Pixley, were among the elite who graced the speedway's program during its waning days of 1934-35. Cole raced in many Indianapolis 500's and ended his career in 1949.

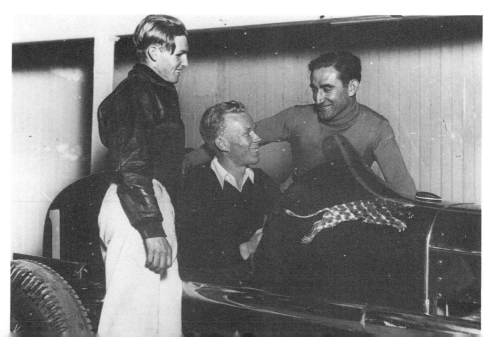

Rex Mays, Ernie Triplett and Al Gordon, left to right, were prominent contenders at the Legion Ascot Speedway. Triplett went east for the 1933 Indy 500, but upon his return found Mays and Gordon as the "head men" at Ascot. Ernie's title was in jeopardy, however. Al took it all that year. Ernie is seated in Art Sparks' car in which Gordon won the 1933 title.

REMEMBERING . . .

(Because the racing escapades of these former Ascot drivers are not fully detailed in the text, these men, however, are listed in recognition of their participation in Ascot racing events. Some are known to be living, but the vast majority remain unaccounted for. Hopefully we have excluded none from the list.)

Let us remember:

Tex Peterson, A. J. Walker, Cliff Ogden, Danny Oakes, Jack Petticord, Lloyd Vieux, Duke Dinsmore, Clyde Bloomgren, Noel Bullock, Bob Sall, Cliff Bergere, Vic Felt, Mauri Rose, Cliff Wilson, Art Boyce, Freddie Agabashian, Barney Kloepfer, Hal Robson, Floyd Davis, Bruce Denslow, Tommy Cosman, Pat Cunningham, Bill Lipscomb, Fred Winnai, Ora Bean, Jimmy Wilkinson, Clarence Langlo, Earl Mansell, Bayliss Leverett, Stan Hallett, Louie Webb, Ray Gardner, Harry Lester, Jack Dinsmoor, Louie Durant, Ellis Bermuda, Johnny Kluckman, Charley Robertson, Manuel Saurez, M. C. Gleason, Clay Buschman, Al Chasteen, P. LaMorr, Les Dreisbach, L. E. Crabtree, L. D. Sullivan, Val Lancaster, Bill Paige, Sam Hoffman, Jimmy McDonald, Ken Baker, Sam Wade, Floyd Sparks, Clarence Peterson, Dean Beach, Pierre Bertrand, Ray Cocking, Russ Del Dotto, Norman Muir, Lane Curry, Jack Webb, Charlie Cyr, Ralph Gregg, Fred Cooper, Paul Barrett, Floyd Stump, Mel Miller, Al Meniam, Pete Neilson, Guy Deulin, Sonny Gleason, Art Hines, Pete Nosik, Gene Woodford, Bud Hyatt, Ed Moody, Bill Bundy, M. O. Babb, Bob Scovel, Earl Hovenden, Joe Kifowit, Tony Radetich, Dewey Skipworth, G. L. Smith, Woody Woodford, Carl Bond, Ed Walker, Charley Oxenfeld, Jimmy Miller, Roy Balaam, Bill Hart, Frank James, Earl Brentlinger, Bob Austin, Bob Gragg, Bill Harper, Ray Durling, Louie Ulbrich, Wirt Stanley, C. C. Oldfield, Robert Bryan, Clarence Downing, E. B. Moody, Leroy Hoag, W. C. Prentiss, Dino Massenelli, Snapper Garrison, Nick Guglielmi, George Robson, Sam Hoffman, Bill Metheny, Ray Dashbrook.

Let's also remember . . .

The following car owners (exclusions are unintentional) :

Tom Mahoney, R. C. Schwerin, Eddie Gates, Fred Frame, Lou Moore, Russ Garnant, Guy Deulen, Bill Rasor, Leo Champion, Bill White, Paul Weirick, Art Sparks, Walt Harris, Ted Simpson, Chad McClerg, Paul Fromm, Earl Haskell, Joe Marks, Kent A. Watson, Arthur Martinson, Ernie Pratt, Kay Tye, Joe Zottarelli, Leo Monson, J. D. Gordon, S. M. Newmark, Willie Utzman, Walt Woestman, C. M. Mikkelson, Ralph Griffin, Roy Bannister, Cliff Wilson, Jack Edwards, J. D. Imbeau, Jack Duffy, Bud Winfield, R. C. Chappell, Russ Chabot, Al Tisnerat, Al Belhalovek, Sam Pintarrelli, Clarence Felker, H. D. Lester, Ed Winfield, Al Morales, Henry Puckett, Jack Taylor, C. R. Wilson, I. A. Trene, Hap Hafferly, Hatton Purdy, Jack Rand, H. J. Hoffman, Henry Stevens, Hilt Tupman, Barbara Worley, T. McBride, Burton Fluke, Gil Pearson, Vince Conze, Lee Morrison, Bill Lipscomb, John Mize, Al Sower, M. Sutoff, Phil Marrow, Darwin Maxson, Curley Record, Doug Taylor, John McDowell, Bielch Brothers, H. J. Hoffman, Jack Rand, J. L. Couch, Art Frost, Lloyd Vieux, Harry Hooker, Francis Quinn, C. H. Bobby, Billy Arnold, Tom Craddock, Curley Grandell, I. M. Hunter, Clarence Langlo, C. C. Ballanger.

INDEX

Ascot Speedway, 1924-1936, where many daredevils risked life and limb to achieve high speed racing glory. (Encircled is the "Lucero-Donahue-Zaldatte tree," where we and other kids witnessed many a thriller when we couldn't sneak in). Below: "Ascot today." School, industrial buildings and houses are on the site where the speedway situated. Hilly roadway is Multnomah Avenue, proceeding towards Wilson High School. (Residential-industrial photo by Mike Sergieff, L.A. Herald-Examiner.)